PRAISE FOR
FOLLOW WITH REASON

"*Follow with Reason* is an invaluable primer for anyone seeking knowledge and empowerment when it comes to understanding and disciplining our natural instinct to follow. It should be required reading for all and kept as a reminder to 'use your head.'"

—**JOHN SCHUSTER,** entrepreneur; Founder and
CEO of American Trainco (now TPC Training)

"Bob presents an interesting perspective on the often taboo topic of following and offers a new and insightful spin to organizational management."

—**DR. AMY KEMTER,** DSW, LCSW-S

"Bob presents an interesting perspective on how following might be a discipline to study further. This book is a good resource to add to your self-development quiver!"

—**ROBERT L. MASON, PhD,** Fellow and former President,
American Statistical Association; Fellow,
American Society for Quality; author

"Bob Galindo's book, *Follow with Reason*, affirms our greatest human capacity as leaders and followers: 'You are not one or the other. You are always both.' His words, supported by research and everyday examples, introduce a paradigm shift in our culture's understanding of true leadership. The author illustrates a positive portrait of *following*, challenging our culturally ingrained negative views. Then, he offers supportive, nonjudgmental advice, providing us with engaging examples of his own hard-earned lessons in learning how to follow with reason."

—**PATTI KOO,** MPAS, PA, advocate and leader,
SNAP (Survivors Network of Those
Abused by Priests), San Antonio, TX

FOLLOW

with

REASON

FOLLOW

MASTERING
THE **5** DEGREES
OF SKILLED
FOLLOWSHIP

with

REASON

BOB GALINDO JR.

RIVER GROVE
BOOKS

Published by River Grove Books
Austin, TX
www.rivergrovebooks.com

Distributed by River Grove Books

Design and composition by Greenleaf Book Group
Cover design by Greenleaf Book Group
Cover images used under license from ©Adobestock.com

Publisher's Cataloging-in-Publication data is available.

Print ISBN: 978-1-63299-941-2

eBook ISBN: 978-1-63299-942-9

First Edition

Dedicated to my mom and dad,
Erma Tudyk Galindo and Roberto Galindo.
And to you. Oh that I can make a positive difference
in at least one person's life today . . .

CONTENTS

PREFACE

Leaders come in many forms: Some are crafty, some are brave, and some are innovative. You may know leaders who are charismatic or determined. Maybe they are good with people or perhaps they are mean, pushy bullies. They might even be lucky and seem like they were born into it. But in my experience, there is a common denominator: Leaders are *followers*. They are simply followers who happen to be in leadership positions. That may seem contradictory, but it is the very thesis of this book. *We are all born followers for life.* From fads of the moment to ideals that span generations, from our parents to our heroes, we must follow something or someone—anyone. It is almost as if we are called to it, as if we are driven to follow.

I am a troubleshooter. A problem-solver. A seeker of resolution. It may sound funny, but I think middle children are quite often forced into this role by default. Stereotypically speaking, middle kids must mediate, compromise, and are often left alone to figure things out for themselves. I don't care. I love it. Besides being a troubleshooting brother, I was a troubleshooting aviation electrician in the navy, a troubleshooting financial officer of a Fortune 100 company, and a troubleshooting dad—all the things. One of my go-to troubleshooting tools in my toolbox is to ask myself, *How was it done in the past? I'll follow their lead.* I don't remember who taught me this tactic of leveraging prior work. My gut just told me to find out if someone else, at some other time, had already done the work of solving the issue for me.

You've probably had similar experiences of running into problems you didn't know the solutions to and finding exactly the right answer online after a little trial and error (and maybe wading through a few pages of nonsense). Seeking and conveying solutions to and from each other—following and being followed—in this way is the cornerstone of generational knowledge. This routine of following is *taught to us.* From one generation to the next, down through the centuries, we have followed and built upon each other's knowledge. In turn, others have followed and built upon our shared knowledge. This is the reason complex mathematics is possible, why modern medicine exists, and why you can buy and use a smartphone without personally understanding how to build and code one. None of these things would be possible without walking in others' footsteps. Not simply learning but *following—with reason.* Learning alone does not create a reasoned follower. A great deal of smart, learned people obeyed Hitler (a follower in his own right). They followed *without* reason.

Those who learn how to grow and master their followership skills come to understand that leading and following are never mutually exclusive. You are not one or the other. In fact, you are always both. This is an observable fact of human nature, as is the fact that high-quality leaders are, in truth, high-quality followers. The art of *skilled followship*, and thus *skilled leadership*, is something that can be taught. But while the basic elements of following are taught to us all, both directly and indirectly, I have not yet found a context in which following *with reason* is taught intentionally. The goal of this book it to begin a dialogue around this gaping hole in our cultural consciousness.

Learning how to follow with reason is more complicated than it first appears. After I retired in 2018, I started looking more seriously into the idea of followership. It was easy for me to understand why, centuries ago, people were inclined to follow *without* reason. After all, at that time, many people were uneducated and illiterate. It is hard to be a critical thinker when you are illiterate, your exposure to new ideas is very limited, and so much of your time is spent on basic survival. Back then, you had little choice but to simply trust what others told you. But now, given the radical increase in literacy—not to mention the increased access to and democratization of information over the last one hundred years—you would think the human tendency to follow without reason would have diminished. But no. In fact, we are as gullible as ever.

It is possible that the impulse to thoughtlessly follow has been amplified by the advent of social media. More than ever, we are succumbing to our addiction to "following" and being "followed," without so much as a second thought. Additionally, growing political polarization on an international scale seems to have made the issue more pronounced. But if it is true that we go along blindly even more in the modern age than we did in the past, the question remains: Why do we follow without reason?

To understand why, you must first embrace the reality that we are all born followers and that no matter what rank you achieve, what success you obtain, or what power you possess, you will remain a follower for life. This is not an insult. It is not inherently a bad thing to be a follower—it is a natural one. But like many natural things, it can, and must, be tamed through will and discipline. To learn to follow with reason, first you must establish a discipline for yourself. All people, even those we call *leaders*, follow. But the best leaders have cultivated the discipline it takes to follow *well* by using their reason. They have mastered an essential set of followership skills. And believe me, the best leaders want the best followers: those who, like them, have also mastered following with reason.

So, what are these followship skills? How can you cultivate them through discipline? And once you've mastered them, how can you maintain and exercise them in service of your goals? Let's start the dialogue.

INTRODUCTION

YOU ARE A
BORN FOLLOWER

When I was a high school freshman, I was in the school band and choir. Through those activities, I made a friend who was a junior and very popular in both groups. I looked up to him as a friend and mentor. One day he asked me, "Do you trust me?" In retrospect, of course that should have been a red flag. But I was a child, really, barely fifteen years old. Eager to follow and to be included (for fear of missing out), I said, "Yes!" He went even further: "You can't tell anyone. No one. No friends. Not even your parents." As an adult, by now you may envision being at a railroad crossing and the bells and flashing red lights are screaming, "Don't cross!" But for me, at that time, all that my little follower mind was thinking was that I'd better hurry up and follow this guy—who was a child himself. I wanted to follow. And I did.

Later, one day after school, well after everyone had left for the day, he led me down to the band hall in the basement, where the entire space was empty and quiet. We went into a small soundproof practice room—maybe ten feet by ten feet—where a single chair was situated. He told me to sit down, with my back to the door, and that the band director would come in. The director came in from behind and blindfolded me. Weird, right?! I thought, *Is this a "pin the tail on the donkey" thing?* But I trusted him; after all, he was my teacher and a consecrated religious figure. And I trusted the older friend I had followed down there. Still, my heart was beating a little faster now. Then he tied my hands behind my back. They were tied loosely, but still, now my heart was racing! Then, before I could say anything, he reached around from behind, held my forehead, and suffocated me with chloroform. Yeah—you read that right: The band director blindfolded me, tied me up, and suffocated me with chloroform. I struggled for a few seconds, heart pounding, legs flailing about, my head and shoulders shaking back and forth, until I passed out. What happened from there you can guess yourself or not; it really doesn't matter. The point of the story is what can happen when you blindly follow. And we all do it more often than we would care to admit. Yes, even you. And the following doesn't cease after childhood.

Failing to Follow and Learning to Lead

Like me, you are a born follower. I say again: *You* are a born follower. Even if it feels uncomfortable or sounds like an insult, it's true. Here's another truth: You will die a follower, too. But don't worry, you're not alone. Every single one of us is born to follow. The sooner we come to grips with this simple fact, the better. This may feel like a hill too high to climb for some of us because our entire lives we have been told *not* to be a follower. We've been conditioned to avoid being seen as a follower, to reject the idea of "being a sheep."

So, naturally, we seek out ways to lead. How many leadership courses have you attended? In my thirty-plus years in the investment advisory industry, I've lost count of the number and types of leadership courses I've attended. I've lost count, and that number is probably higher than my best guess. With so many options, they must get creative with names: not just "courses" or "training" anymore, but also "workshops," "seminars," "webinars," and "retreats." That's not even counting the leadership books available. Most leadership books rely on historical examples to guide future leaders, advocating for what you should follow in the future based on the strength of what has worked in the past.

Nevertheless, regardless of the tack they take, in my opinion these books all teach the same thing in different words and phrases: a Top 10 list, a building-block pyramid, the new leadership fad, and so on. Often, they conflate the concept of leadership with related but distinct ideas, such as decision-making, ingenuity, entrepreneurship, charisma, or strength of character (sometimes conflated with bullying). The industry even resurrects old leadership methods. Are you familiar with the idea of "servant leadership"? It might be the trend today, but the concept is thousands of years old, with roots in Islamic and Confucian ideology.[1] Lao Tzu, an ancient Chinese philosopher of the fifth century BC, is often cited as writing, "A leader is best when people barely know he exists . . . when his work is done, his aim fulfilled, they will all say: 'We did it ourselves.'" And, of course, Christians will point to the words of Jesus:

> *You know that those who are recognized as rulers*
> *over the Gentiles lord it over them, and their*
> *great ones make their authority over them felt.*
> *But it shall not be so among you. Rather, whoever*
> *wishes to be great among you will be your servant;*
> *whoever wishes to be first among you will be the*
> *slave of all. For the Son of Man did not come*
> *to be served but to serve and to give his life as*
> *ransom for many.*[2]

Servant leadership is just one of many leadership tropes filling bookstore shelves. Did you know that, according to the Business Research Company, the corporate training industry is estimated to be $401 billion globally in 2024 at a compound annual growth rate (CAGR) of 4.6 percent?[3] GlobeNewswire estimates the subset of that global training market, global leadership training, to be $63 billion by 2030, as reported in *Fortune Business Insights*.[4] Please note those amounts are billions, with a *B*! It's no wonder there is a constant flow of new or resurrected ideas and forums. At any rate, they all fail to produce lasting results. Do you ever wonder why? It is because they all ignore one simple fact: Every single one of us is a born follower—for life.

Following Is Central to Capitalism

Despite the collective *need* to follow, we don't like the idea. We certainly don't like the word, at least in the United States, which is very odd considering that following is a core tenant of capitalism. Think of *equilibrium*. In economic terms, this is where the market attempts to find a balance between supply and demand. If a company has a product or service and they are its only producer, the supply is less than demand. The result is a large profit. So, the theory of capitalism says that others will follow that profit generator and get into the game. They will follow the profit maker and become a supplier of the same or a very similar product, thereby adding to the supply chain and availing themselves of some of that profit. To the extent that supply meets demand, the profit level comes down and there is equilibrium.

The principle is the same on the demand side of the equation. It may be easier to understand my point from this approach because it has to do with the purchaser—and we are all purchasers, are we not? The demand side of equilibrium comes with a bit of marketing psychology to get people to follow, yet we don't call it "following" in that case. However you look at it, businesses utilize marketing to create, support, or otherwise coerce people into following, thereby increasing demand. They do this by selling an idea, by attaching products to our values and desires, which leads us to purchase products that millions of others also own. Businesses follow successful businesses; people purchase popular goods and services. Following is everywhere.

The irony is that we are taught competing messages. One message says to buck the trends, to be a leader. The competing message teaches us to follow the status quo. For example, when we see that someone has a cool gadget or service, we become part of the demand function of the equilibrium equation by following their lead. We follow . . . without reason. Remember when your mom or dad would ask you, "Would you follow your friend if they jumped off a cliff?" From the earliest of ages, those born in the United States are taught to ignore or fight against this thing you do so naturally every day. You may even feel compelled to outright *deny* that it happens to you, which is worse—potentially dangerous, even. Think of how propaganda preys on your instinct to follow.

Yet, at the same time, following was taught to you, wasn't it? Our society institutionalizes following beginning at a very young age. I recall songs from my childhood about following the leader, made especially memorable in Disney's animated *Peter Pan*, watched by millions of children. A quick internet search for "follow the leader songs for children" yields tens of millions of results. We may wish to brush these off as simply childish songs, but one must admit it is only one of several tools in our toolbox that we employ to teach following at home, in school, and in society. The thing is, we omit the need to teach our children to follow *with reason*. This can be very dangerous, as illustrated by my personal story at the beginning of the book.

Regardless of the paradox of those messages, where we are told to be a leader but taught to be a follower, following is not inherently bad. It can be very good and very fruitful. Following helps keep things organized; it decreases chaos. We follow to be a part of a group, a team, an organization, a community, city, state, nation, and so on. It is a topic well documented by the scientific community. For example, we begin to respond to noises and voices after about twenty-five to twenty-six weeks of gestation.[5]

Not long after we are born, our eyes track movements.[6] When we crawl, we follow our parents or siblings. We follow the leader in childhood games. We learn to follow instructions at home and at school. As adults, we "follow in someone's footsteps."

Even kids can generate followers. I remember being a kid, maybe ten or twelve, waiting for a bus in downtown San Antonio with my older cousins. One of them started looking up at the top of a building. He wasn't pointing, and he wasn't saying anything. "What are you looking at?" I asked. He answered, "Nothing. It doesn't matter, just look up and watch. All the other people will start looking up." So, I did. And he was right! Everyone else did too. And for the record, this took place at a city bus stop, not a school bus stop. Those were *adults* following children.

We All Want a Following

The other side to this instinctual drive to follow is the drive to want to *be followed*. In my previous example, my cousin wanted to be followed. He wouldn't have been looking up for very long if people didn't mimic his lead. Where's the fun in that? Perhaps an example more people are familiar with is the story that inspired *Les Misérables*, the 1862 novel by Victor Hugo that has been made into a musical, various plays, and movies. The main storyline concerns the redemption of a former convict, named

Jean Valjean. But what concerns us here is the side story of the June Rebellion, also called the Paris Uprising of 1832. The author accurately retells the story of a group of young revolutionaries who set up barricades in Paris following the death of General Lamarque, who was critical of the monarchy of the time. These young people, outnumbered at least ten to one, stood no chance of winning—and they knew it. But their strong conviction was that people would follow them. They wanted to be followed. Though they all perished in the uprising, their martyrdom led to a subsequent cultural influence that succeeded—one that would not have been possible without those followers.[7]

There is a comfort in being followed. A feeling of affirmation overcomes you when people get behind you and support your words or actions. Our political leaders are the most obvious examples of those who want to be followed. If they find they are not, often, they change their political position. It is almost as if, in the back of our brains, we know that everyone else has the instinct to follow as well. Nevertheless, are we *cognizant* of our natural-born instinct to follow? Do we have and do we utilize good *skills* to follow well? What *are* good followership skills?

This is not a leadership book, although it *could* be. It is not an academic book, although there is academic support behind its thesis. It is not a political or religious book, although examples for following abound in those arenas too. My aim here is to focus on something else: to explore this aspect of our lives as humans that is fundamental but often neglected. Let's start a discussion. The thesis to consider here is that *following* is in our DNA, our genes. In a manner of speaking, it is root-of-the-brain kind of stuff.

To follow, to be a follower, to be following—this is an instinct we are all born with, and it never leaves us. Religious leaders and politicians know this all too well. Scientists and academics are experts at it, going so far as to make the task of developing detailed documents for others to follow a key element of their craft. But marketing and political professionals—oh, these geniuses know about our following default better than nearly anyone else. Now, in the digital and mobile global communication age, where it is almost impossible to escape the seemingly endless propaganda, marketing, and data-generating-and-harvesting business objectives, and especially when considering the adaptation of artificial intelligence, it is more important than ever to develop tools to help you be a self-disciplined, *trained* follower. Someone who "follows with reason": *sequi cum ratione*.

A Scientific Framework for Followship

In the 1930s, Austrian Nobel Prize–winning zoologist and ethologist Konrad Lorenz performed experiments with geese showing that "imprinting" causes newly hatched geese to form an attachment with the first moving thing they see.[8] The principle that he was *following* was documented one hundred years earlier by Douglas Spalding, but "imprinting" sounds better than "following."

The work done by Spalding and Lorenz has been replicated since and expanded to prove that it applies to humans.[9] Now we call it "attachment theory," "attachment bias," or "attachment disorder." There are several forms of attachment theory as it relates to humans, but at the root of any attachment is the instinct to follow, not just physically, but mentally and emotionally, and perhaps even spiritually.[10] Humans, as with other animals, have this instinct. Then we reinforce it by teaching each other to follow. And it works. It seems like a circular formula, does it not? We are born to follow and then we teach others to follow.

When this following phenomenon is studied in business or political arenas, it is still not identified as "following." If the word is used at all in those contexts, it is intentionally delivered as an insult: "They just follow blindly," or "They are the blind following the blind." This is what many people say about the opposing political side, not realizing that they, too, are following. In fact, there's a well-known name for this phenomenon: "groupthink."

Psychologist Irving Janis, building on the work of others before him, popularized the term *groupthink* in the 1970s.[11] In Janis's case, it was the work of William Whyte Jr. in the 1950s, who came up with the term *groupthink*, referring to "rationalized conformity."[12] Before Whyte, there was George Orwell's "doublethink," as presented in his 1949 dystopian novel, *1984*. Janis applied the theory to the political events of his time, specifically President John F. Kennedy and the failed Bay of Pigs invasion, then the Vietnam War.[13] Sometime later, the idea of groupthink was used to help explain the *Challenger* space shuttle disaster.[14] Simply put, *groupthink* is another word for *following*. Some may call it *conformity*. Wait long enough and someone will come up with another reformulation of the same idea. And we will all respond, "Yep, makes sense to me," most likely because the person next to us said, "Yep, that makes sense to me."

As an example, take the gestalt (study of perception) psychologist Solomon Ashe's experiments from the 1950s on conformity.[15] The experiment consisted of showing a small test group of college students two cards. One card had a line drawn on it of a particular length. The other card had three lines on it—one line being the same length as the line on the first card, a line materially shorter, and one line materially longer. Only one person in the group was the test subject. The other men in the group (it was the '50s, so only men were allowed) were actors, and they were given instructions on how to answer the question, "Which line on the second card is the same length as the line on the first card?" Over a series of testing scenarios, where sometimes the actors answered correctly and sometimes incorrectly, but always in unison, the results showed that only 25 percent of the time the test subject consistently stayed with the correct answer rather than joining the incorrect majority. But more than 35 percent of the time, the test subject consistently went with the majority *incorrect* answer.

Ashe's test showed that individuals are likely to go along with a consensus answer, even when they believe it to be in error. Think about the significance of these results. They go along with a consensus answer, *even when they believe it to be in error.* This is what your mom warned you about when she asked if you'd follow your friend off a cliff. In Ashe's experiments, based on the subjects' response to debriefing questions after the experiment, they might have indicated they made the decision to conform out of a desire to "go with the flow" (normative conformity), or perhaps they considered that they could be or must be short of some relevant information (informative conformity). Or who knows? The variables are almost infinite. Perhaps they had some emotional baggage that led them to follow or "conform." Perhaps it was because they were "men being men"—a factor disproved over the decades with replicated experiments.[16] At any rate, the answer is simple: We are born followers. Let me be clear, though. This human propensity for following the wrong thing is not isolated to following the majority. Depending on the circumstances, people may follow the incorrect answer and justify their choice as a matter of obedience.

Such was the case during the well-known "Milgram Experiment," conducted by social psychologist Stanley Milgram to study human submission to authority.[17] This experiment started in the 1960s and has been replicated in various forms in the decades since.[18] The experiment required the test subjects, who were receiving instructions from an authority figure, to punish an anonymous person with electrical shocks for incorrect answers. The test subject was not literally shocking the third person—that part was staged. There was a wall separating the test subject from the anonymous person, allowing the researchers to create the illusion that the test subject was administering an electrical shock to the person on the other side of the wall. That anonymous person was an actor, who would yell in pain when the test subject administered the electrical shock punishment for an incorrect answer. The intensity of the shock increased each time the anonymous person gave an incorrect answer, which they, of course, were directed to do by the researchers. The objective of the experiment was to determine how far the test subject would go in hurting someone else at the instruction of an authority figure.

There have been many debates over the plethora of variables that make an experiment such as Milgram's difficult to replicate in a controlled manner, in addition to the ethical concerns this type of experiment raises. Nevertheless, the results showed a clear tendency of people to submit to authority and follow orders, even when those orders went against their higher moral standards. Ergo, the desire to follow has the potential to *supersede even cultural morals and standards*. Again, think of the significance of that statement. This is especially important when considering large-scale following patterns in social, religious, political, and military movements.

The irony is that in cases of the many global and historical atrocities committed in the name of obedience, society tends to blame the leaders, because they play a dominant role, but in reality, much boils down to people's simple and innate tendency to follow. Many leaders themselves are moved by their constituents. They, in fact, are the ones being led. Not long ago, Mitch McConnell (R-Ky), Senate minority leader at the time of this writing, was quoted by a *New York Times* reporter saying, "I didn't get to be leader by voting with five people in the conference."[19] So, who is leading who? Who is following who? I understand that science likes answers, and that's a good thing. More research leads to more information, which leads to more nuance. So, the experiments, peer reviews, and replications are all good. But regardless of the specific details, the fact remains that we follow. The real question is: How do we use this to our advantage? Let's get down to it.

1

THE DEGREES OF
FOLLOWSHIP

Back in the '80s, when I was getting my college education, Lee Iacocca was turning around Chrysler Motor Co. As a well-known and well-regarded leader, he was often quoted in popular media. One of the things he said that gained widespread popularity was, "So what do we do? Anything. Something. So long as we just don't sit there. If we screw it up, start over."[1] That idea became a problem for me in my early career.

In the late '90s, I was a junior officer at a large company. I was well versed in my technical craft and knowledge of the industry; I'd been brought into the company for that very reason. But this new company was big, bureaucratic, and old school in its culture, from an operating and interpersonal perspective—in a word, *political.* Think about the stereotypes of IBM in its heyday. At this particular company, so much was dependent upon perception. People who worked there spent much of their time guiding or influencing what people did see or didn't see, directing what people said or didn't say, watching the flow and style of their communication, and the process of decision-making—or lack thereof.

At this company, some people wanted to make a major change with a third-party provider. These people were well connected and flourished in their appearances-focused corporate culture. But they only had about 20 percent use (relationship ownership) of this third-party provider, while my area of responsibility had 80 percent ownership. In addition, my experience and knowledge in this particular area was why I was hired. When I began trying to use reason to explain to these people why changing our third-party provider was a bad idea, I found that I started losing to the political influence of that 20 percent.

Why did they want to make the change? Honestly, I think me coming onboard drew followers away from them, and they felt threatened. I don't believe that they felt a loss of control of ownership of the third party. I believe it was a loss of followers, especially at the senior executive level. As a result, instead of evaluating whether it was actually a problem, they wanted to create some noise and make a change—just to "do something" and draw attention to themselves. It wasn't a reasoned path. In my mind, doing something like this meant the business was going to make a bad decision. I judged that people were following without reason. Some may call this scenario an example of groupthink, but let's call it what it is: *following*. In fact, a senior executive said exactly this to me: "It's not the first time a bad decision has been or will be made here." He was a veteran at this organization. He specifically said, "Just follow. Just do it." I classify this thought process and its subsequent action as that of a *developing follower*. Followers in this degree often follow even when they know it's the wrong thing. They just do it anyway.

But I wasn't satisfied to be a developing follower, so I wouldn't just do it. I put my job and career at this company on the line because I knew that, in this case, following was the wrong thing. It was extremely difficult to push my colleagues to follow reason over immature following. I swear that part of my success in the business world stems from getting people to stop or avoid doing stupid things just for the sake of doing *something*. Don't get me wrong, I respect and admire Mr. Iacocca, and there is something helpful in his idea, but making a wrong decision can also cost more than not acting.

Not acting is not the same as indecision. Not taking a particular path is often viewed as inaction or being obstructionist. This kind of effort is very taxing emotionally, mentally, and physically because you're fighting against people's desire to follow, even if their desire to follow is without reason. Remember, not taking an action *is* a decision. One could say the choice of nonaction is an action, though it is not often perceived that way. Learned followers are those who follow even when they know it's not a good idea. They are "learned" in terms of learning *how* to follow but not in terms of determining with reason *what* or *who* to follow. The senior executive was more of a learned follower in that scenario, and I believe I was more of a curious follower. What was I following? Reason.

Progressing Through the Degrees of Followship

To illustrate my point, I've developed the following chart as a visual guide to the degrees of followship and the path most of us take when we progress from instinctual followers to informed followers to learned followers to curious followers and, finally, to followers who practice vulnerability. This last degree, vulnerability, is slightly more complex than those that precede it, and most people find themselves progressing to it and regressing back again over the course of their lives. Regression is, of course, possible in each of the degrees of followship. Like any pursuit in life, your path through the degrees of followship will be determined by the experiences you acquire and your response to those experiences.

Degrees of Following with Reason

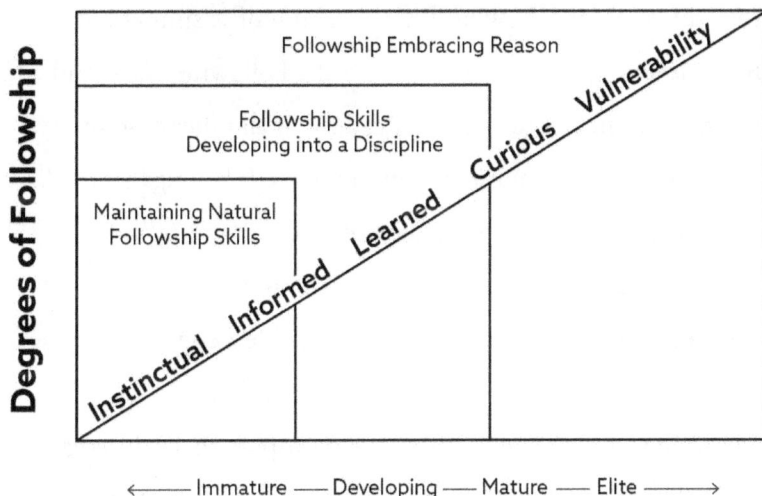

Figure 1.1

Instinctual Following

Do you see how we start off on the left bottom corner? This is the first degree of followship, "instinctual." This is the state of followship we are born into and remain in our entire lives. Do we ever get over our base instincts? No, of course not. The best we can hope for is to acknowledge them and train them. This initial, default state is the "immature" stage of followship. Some call it the "lizard brain." This is a colloquial term used to refer to the basal ganglia and brain stem regions. I simply call it the "root of the brain" or "back of the brain." Instinctually, we need to eat and drink, find shelter, reproduce, and so on. We don't think about these things; we just do them. Some might say that this type of following I am speaking of is simply a means to achieve these base instinctual needs. Following is, in and of itself, a base instinctual need. Meaning, if all other base survival needs are met, we are *still* driven to follow. It belongs on the list of basic needs: eat, drink, shelter, reproduce, and *follow.*

This idea is like psychologist Abraham Maslow's physiological needs stage of human motivation.[2] He defined five stages of human development based on "needs" or "motivation," beginning with physiological needs. I propose that *following* is a physiological need. It does not simply *relate* to back-of-the-brain instinct and basic physiological needs, it *is* one. Like magnets, we are drawn to each other. If you see someone go somewhere to get food and water, odds are you're going to follow them, instinctually, even if you're not hungry. If you *don't* follow them, your body might respond with that gnawing feeling in your gut, signaling that something is amiss. *Why am I alone?*

Perhaps it is what we commonly refer to nowadays as "FOMO"—fear of missing out. We follow people to the entrance of a building even though we may not know if that is the correct entrance. We look up at the sky if someone else is looking up, even though we may not know what we are looking for. Perhaps, somewhere in the recesses of our minds, we are worried about pterodactyls coming to snatch us away. (Recall the bus stop story where adults were following children.) We don't think about it much; we just *do*. The instinct to follow is something you can observe in many other animals: bees, lions, chimpanzees, and bears. It is an intrinsic instinctual drive—no experience necessary. Remember the phrase "Do as I say, not as I do"? Parents are known to use this repeatedly, but why? Because parents know their children will instinctually follow whatever actions they see before them—whether they're age appropriate or not!

Informed Following

Speaking of parents, they are the primary, though not sole, instigators of the second degree of followship: "informed." Parents are the first people to help us sharpen our following instinct. And I would argue that they can't help themselves either. I believe there are back-of-the-brain forces that compel parents to teach their children to follow. I would even go so far as to suggest that *all* adults, whether they have children or not, want to teach children to follow them and their example or advice. And not just children—anyone. Don't you find it difficult to keep your mouth shut sometimes when you have an opinion on how to do things? Or do you want to have a "following" and be followed? We all do. This drive has nothing to do with primordial survival or self-care. You simply can't help yourself, and social media has zeroed in on that instinctual need. Long before the invention of the internet, parents throughout the ages have been trying to accumulate "followers," "likes," and "thumbs-up" from their kids, their parents, their siblings, fellow parents, neighbors, and even strangers.

Our parents want to help us progress from instinctual followship to informed followship and become developing, if still immature, followers. They do this because they have an instinct to teach following. It is at this informed degree of skill development that you embraced *how* to follow. Follow correctly and you get positive feedback—rewarded for simply following. It feels good, and it reinforces your instinct to follow. So, following equals good. At the same time, your ability to comprehend and retain information is separating you from the rest of the animal kingdom. You are able to learn that you can learn. But even in this next stage, where you moved beyond your lizard brain and began using your cognition, you didn't outgrow your instinct to follow, the same way that you didn't outgrow your instinct to eat. Instead, at this informed degree of followship, you build upon and reinforce your already instinctual drive.

As children, we are informed by our parents, school, church, and society at large. This is beyond instinctual or survival followship traits. For example, I remember watching my dad hang up his pants. This will date me some, but did you ever use the type of hangers that would clasp the cuff of your pants, so you'd hang your pants upside down? My dad was very meticulous. He informed me, by his actions, which I simply watched, that hanging up clothes was something we do. It is more basic than learning. To a child, hanging up clothes seems like a lot of work, right? And, to what end? Playing sounds much better, and who cares what you look like anyway? But I followed his example— well, I was *instructed* to follow his example. He informed me of a great number of things beyond the actual task without intending to, I believe. I watched him, listened to him, and followed him, mostly because I instinctually wanted to, but also because I was instructed to do so. Therefore, I learned that following was something we do. Still, there was not a great deal of reasoning happening at this stage, but there was certainly a great deal of being *informed* to follow, supporting the understanding that following was good and natural. That understanding prepares us for moving forward in the progression.

Learned Following

The next degree of followship is "learned." We've progressed from the instinct to understand and need; now we move on to *what* to follow. We have matured and learned. We start to think we are smart. And we are! I am amazed when I consider the limitlessness of the human mind. We can learn math, science, history, art, culture, and religion—and any number of other diverse subjects. Sometimes, this is where we may lose ourselves to overconfidence and ego. We have learned that we have the ability to learn, which is good and natural, but it comes at the expense of *forgetting* that we have an instinct to follow. In doing so, we forget our baseline. Most of us let our followship guard down at this point. We get lazy. Because it feels comfortable, we may not progress from here. This point in our followship journey is akin to the "love and belonging" stage of Maslow's hierarchy of needs. For the record, Maslow also believed that most of us live in this space most of our lives and do not progress further. This complacency happens so slowly we don't realize it.

This stagnation is even worse if the person who has stopped progressing is in some kind of leadership role. Often, their ego takes over and they completely forget that they are also followers. They become stuck in "I know the way and I am right" mode, and the result is that they are inadequate leaders at best, and destructive leaders at worst. In support of their ego, one possible cause of stagnation in this stage is confirmation bias. Confirmation bias is a killer of following with reason. It happens when we search only for data and information that supports our position, excluding from consideration anything that undermines it. At this point we are "learned," and we think that because we are learned, we are *completely knowledgeable*. We do our flawed research, allow confirmation bias to show us what we want to see, and, based on this deeply flawed basis, make our choice of what or who to follow. The confirmation bias supports our ego, which creates a loop that keeps us in this learned degree of followship. It is difficult to bust out. It takes effort and exercise.

I am guilty of this myself when it comes to my personal investments or personal view of the economic environment. If I am set on a stock that I like, or the mood that I think the market or economy is in, I find myself seeking out literature that supports my opinion. I must literally force myself to look for alternate points of view and options. With respect to leadership, I believe that this is a puzzle the leadership training industry is unwittingly trying to solve: what to do with the learned follower. One problem with this approach is that the leadership training industry is attempting to start a *new* puzzle for the individual rather than working to complete the puzzle already in progress. The individual is the puzzle. I suppose the thought is that it would be easier to start a new "leadership" puzzle, meaning to change the person. I don't think it can be done.

We are born followers and are followers for life. I don't believe this part of the puzzle can be changed. But—and this is a *big* but—if we can find a way to break out of the ego–confirmation bias loop that holds many of us in the learned degree of follow-ship and complete the existing puzzle by leveraging our learned follower stage, then we have found the path of a natural leader. And a natural leader is, in reality, an elite follower. The very best leaders do not often need leadership training to get over this confirmation-bias obstacle because they never forget they are followers. More often, they don't even get stuck in this loop to begin with and are naturally moved into the next degree of followership.

Curious Following

The curious black-belt followers are an elite group. The people at this point in their followship development never stop wanting to follow. They search. They admit or surrender to their position as a follower. Admittedly, they don't *call* themselves followers—that would be taboo—but they act like them. People who maintain a curious relationship to followship hunger and thirst for knowledge. They look for alternatives, challenges, examples. They wonder and they ask questions. They look for relationships between ideas. Scientists are some of the best followers, and they know it! A pillar of this discipline is creating a detailed recipe, leaving repeatable instructions for those who follow. They follow and, moreover, they want to be followed, want their experiments to be replicated. If you were to look up any of the academics mentioned in this book, any Nobel Prize winner, you will find in their biography a list of people they have followed.

The level of curiosity exemplified by the best followers is typified by reading. How much do you read? What do you read? Why do you read? Reading, by definition, is an exercise in following with reason. The ability to read and write, to use a baking metaphor (or the compounding effect in finance), acts like yeast, in that both assist in the growth of knowledge and understanding and, therefore, following with reason. While verbal transfer of knowledge degrades with each iteration (think the "telephone" or "pass the message" game), writing does not and as a result, reading has a multiplying effect via its clarity and permeance. It takes following to another level by introducing an accurate and permanent record—something that can be referenced and tested. Reading is fundamental to following with reason.

One example of a well-known leader who was a voracious, curious reader was Albert Einstein. Marie Curie, the first person to win two Nobel Prizes, is another.[3] Abraham Lincoln taught himself how to read (saw someone else reading, no doubt, and followed their example).[4] Most US presidents who are viewed as having made a historically positive impact were well read; the most notable may be Thomas Jefferson and Theodore Roosevelt.[5] Those who were not well read—well, I'd say that they were probably not the best leaders. Then there is Winston Churchill, Margaret Thatcher, Queen Elizabeth I, and Mahatma Gandhi.[6] Most great military generals were avid readers. Business leaders of our generation include Warren Buffet, who is said to spend 80 percent of his day reading, Bill Gates, Oprah Winfrey, Elon Musk, and Jeff Bezos.[7]

Vulnerable Following

There is, finally, the pinnacle degree of followship attained by very few: "vulnerability." It involves a mastery of fear and level of humility that few people can achieve and even fewer are able to sustain. Why would a reasoned follower need vulnerability? One might think this attribute would lead to *unreasoned* following because, quite often, it is associated with weakness—a baby is vulnerable—or one may describe a vulnerable adult as "without a spine." Dr. Brené Brown has done some excellent work in this space and authored several books, including *Daring Greatly* and *Dare to Lead*, in which she identifies emotions such as shame and fear as being inhibitors to bravery and courage, calling out being vulnerable as being a tool to overcome these emotions (shame, fear, bravery, courage).

I would add, though, that it is the stoic approach, not emotional, that is at the essence of reasoned vulnerability as a degree of followship. It is a virtue. One cannot eliminate emotion from our brain process. We think emotion comes from our gut—it does not. All of this happens in our brain. This is a good thing because we can train our brain. Though very different, emotion and reason are complementary gifts that we can use in our life as a sort of checks and balances. It is difficult to keep emotion in check with another emotion. Still, emotion remains, but not necessarily in a bad way. Most noble leaders, known and unknown, approach vulnerability as a strength. Even our American founding fathers utilized this approach in their lives and as a building block of our country. Jeffrey Rosen (current president and CEO of the National Constitution Center), in *The Pursuit of Happiness*, discusses stoic reasoning (following the example of Greek and Roman philosophers) as the basis for "being good, not feeling good."[8] Being good is the reasoned approach. Feeling good is the emotion.

One of the best examples of this reasoned vulnerability as a virtue is witnessed in the life of Jesus. You don't have to be a Christian to understand my point, just know the story. It is one of virtue and humility in the presence of suffering, all in the service of others; Jesus *following* his Father (God), with reason, to his death for the benefit of others. It is simply remarkable.

One might conclude that God, the creator of the universe, could change everything according to His will with a simple word. Yet, in these Gospel stories, God chooses to become man and to submit Himself to death by crucifixion.[9] To what end? In the Gospels, it is for the salvation of humanity, which, again, He could have done with a word. Perhaps the end goal was to teach humanity this very lesson of active vulnerability—desiring that we would choose to *follow with reason*—vulnerability in action.

Nevertheless, the example is fitting for following with reason; self-sacrificial service *following* a greater good. USAA, a highly regarded major financial services company, has this as a motto: "We know what it means to serve." Having worked there myself, I know that the company goes to great lengths to create a culture of vulnerability. I don't remember it ever being discussed in such terms, but the mission of service at the expense of self is at the center. This is the degree of vulnerability that I am aiming to illustrate in this book. "Do nothing out of selfishness or out of vainglory; rather, humbly regard others as more important than yourselves, each looking out not for his own interest, but everyone for those of others."[10] This is reasoned vulnerability.

Regardless of whether you are a "successful" or "failed" follower—depending upon your definitions of *success* and *failure*—you still follow. Like leadership, following is different from having good or bad followership *skills*. In other words, you can be a successful leader or a failed leader, but you are still a leader so long as you have a leadership role. One can be a very good and eager follower but have a deficit of followship *skills*, resulting in poor decisions, like saying, "Yes, ma'am, I am indeed going to follow my friend over a cliff because I am the best follower *ever*!"

Being a good and eager follower *without* followship skills can lead to undesired or harmful consequences. By the same token, *refusing* to follow when you should, when it is the reasoned decision, or choosing *not* to follow due to reasons of pride or some rebellious desire is equally harmful and unreasonable (i.e., teenagers resisting following their parents just to rebel). The same reasoning applies for following from one thing to another, such as applying the reasoning process you use in deciding to follow a sports team to following a political leader or ideal. They are two completely different things requiring two different avenues of reasoning.

Remember: Refusing to follow one thing always means you are following something else. Having a deficit of followship skills doesn't mean you *do not* follow. Everyone follows. It just means you do not follow well or wisely. In Latin, *sequi sin ratione* means "follow without reason." What would we rather do? *Sequi cum ratione* or "follow with reason"? It is all about identifying and taming a followship skill set. Figure 1.2 illustrates this dynamic.

Followship Skill Level vs. Following off a Cliff

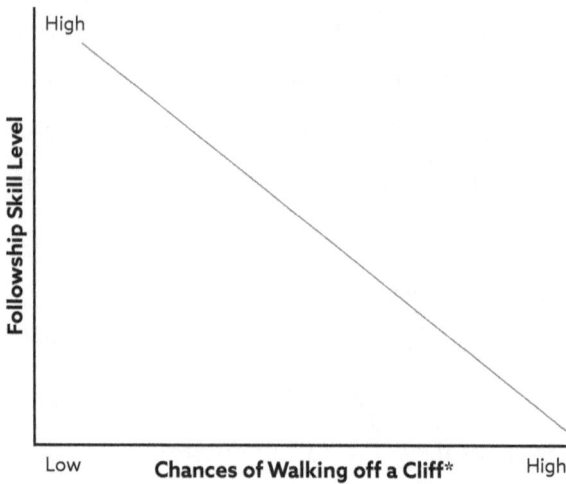

*Disposition to conform to authority, submit to manipulation, or desire
to be part of the group

Figure 1.2

No matter where you fall on the graph, you are following because you can't help it—you were born to follow. But if you don't develop good followship skills, you will *sequi sin ratione*—follow without reason—and willingly or blindly go over a cliff.

A Few Words on Leadership

Some say, "To be a good leader, you have to learn to follow first." What the "learn to follow first" phrase is really trying to convey is submission and conformity, as one might find at a military boot camp, for example. This saying reduces, and even cheapens, the role of following to the game of "follow the leader" that you played as a kid. It implies blind, unreasoned following. And that once you are placed in a leadership role, you cease to follow. To make matters worse, as a leader with this mindset, you demand unreasoned followers. People who ascribe to this way of thinking are ineffective leaders, at best. At worst, these people can be dangerous. The statement does get something right, however, which is the "learn" part. You must *learn* to follow *well—with reason.*

I am not talking about that kind of blind submission or surrender to authority. I am talking about *skills*. If you don't have good followship skills, you are likely a terrible leader. I believe the military knows this and teaches it, if obscurely. They call leaders "people with authority."[11] In a military context, even generals are followers.[12] Being a leader or in a leadership position does not let you off the hook of working to obtain a higher level of followship skills or to exercise and hone those skills. People with low followship skills, whether in a leadership position or not, are subject to all the labels we discussed: conformity, abusive authority, manipulation, ineptitude, and so on, even when they are in a leadership role. The pyramid chart shows the evolution of the degrees of followship.

Followship Degrees

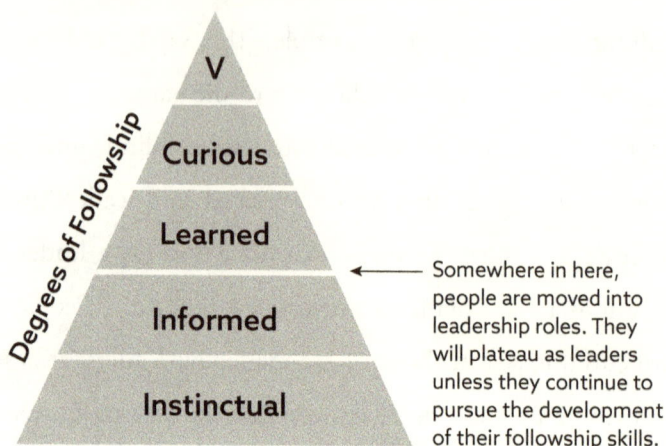

V is for vulnerability—physical, mental, and emotional vulnerability; the pinnacle of an elite follower.

Figure 1.3

The progression along the degrees of followship is fluid. We can and do move forward and backward within any given degree and between degrees. It may seem as though we leave one degree and move on to another after we have mastered that particular part of the journey, but no one really ever moves past the instinctual level. In fact, quite the opposite. The building within this degree occurs in mastering the knowledge that we have always had that instinct within us. Therein lies the reason why this level requires lifelong attention. The same is true in the "informed" degree, where we are instructed how to follow. Have you heard the expression "lifelong learner"? Hopefully, we all aspire to this goal. Here again, the growth occurs in making a discipline of exercising certain attributes within this degree. And so it goes with the remaining degrees: "learned," "curious," and "vulnerable." In the following chapters, we will dive into each degree and the attributes that serve best as starting points for us in our quest to follow with reason.

TAKEAWAYS

- There are **degrees of following with reason** (followship), and your goal is to become aware of them and discipline them as you grow.

- The first degree of followship is **instinctual**—this is the state in which you are born and in which you retain (not remain) as a foundation. It is a basic instinct, like the need for food or sleep.

- The next degree of followship is **informed**. At this point, your parents and those around you (society) help you **understand that following is necessary, good, and natural**. It reinforces your instinct to follow.

- The next degree of following is **learned**. At this point, most of you have **acquired some experiences and gained knowledge**. But this knowledge can trick you into thinking that you are no longer a follower. **Many** people become stuck at this stage—following without reason. This complacency can be very dangerous.

- In the next degree of followship, **curious** followers never stop wanting to follow. They put thought (reason) into it. People who **maintain a curious relationship to followship hunger and thirst for knowledge.**

- The final degree of followship is practicing **vulnerability**. It is stoic reason, not emotion, that is at the essence of reasoned vulnerability as a degree of followship. It is a virtue involving the mastery **of fear and a level of humility that few people are able to achieve**, and even fewer are able to sustain. "Do nothing out of selfishness or vainglory; rather, humbly regard others as more important than yourselves."[13]

- Followship skills are important to cultivate at every point along the way because **having a deficit of followship skills doesn't mean you do not follow.** *Everyone* follows. It just means you do not follow well or wisely—with reason.

2

INSTINCTUAL

We all have an instinctual drive to follow. There is scientific evidence supporting this claim, gathered from more than a century's worth of research and experimentation—from Spalding and Lorenz on imprinting, to Ashe and others on conformity, to Milgram on submission to authority. There is also anthropological evidence spanning the history of mankind—following gods, nature, the elements, the stars, etc.—right up to Janus's thoughts on groupthink, leaving little doubt that we are born with this instinct. Given the evidence, admitting this instinct exists is the first hurdle to overcome in our journey through the degrees of followship. Don't let pride get in the way! In the process of coming to grips with this reality, pride can derail the whole endeavor. We have no hope of mastering the instinct degree of followship, and therefore the entire path of reasoned following, if we cannot get over this first hurdle. Accepting the knowledge that we are all followers requires surrendering our pride, and perhaps also our fear. This is difficult, I grant you that.

I have some personal experience with surrendering pride and fear that I can share, so you can understand the extent to which I'm aware of how difficult this first hurdle can be. My hope is that I will also emphasize the concept of following as a baseline behavior we are born with and must admit to. I have a chronic brain disease, a substance abuse disorder. The specifics of it are inconsequential for this example, but let's call it alcoholism if that helps pin things down. It is my baseline. I was born this way. It is unmovable, unchangeable. If I went through my life ignoring that reality and letting my baseline tendency toward addiction have its way with me, it would lead to me making some very poor choices. I have learned first, and most importantly, that this is my baseline.

It took me decades to surrender to this reality. An important point for me in accepting this was the science. When I investigated the science that I present throughout this book, the truth of my condition became evident. This knowledge continues to help me understand and manage this baseline I have. There is science behind it: neuroscience, behavioral science, and so on. I have learned that there are some tools—a skill set, a discipline set—to help me manage this baseline, perhaps even to leverage it to good use. I can master it, rather than let it master me. But I'm sure you've heard that the first step to recovery is admitting your baseline. I use this example to illustrate that *following* is your baseline—and one of mine—and though the hurdle of surrendering your pride and fear is high, you must make that leap and admit that following is your baseline. It is the first step to recovery and, eventually, to mastery.

After admitting we're all followers by instinct, the next step is to take yourself out of the equation and develop self-awareness. How often have you heard the phrase, "He thinks the world revolves around him"? The truth is that it applies to everyone, irrespective of gender, ethnicity, age, or socioeconomic status. Some people who repeat that phrase, criticizing others for thinking the world revolves around them, are saying so only because they are frustrated that the world is not currently revolving around *them* instead. Lately, the word *narcissist* has become a widely used label and is often loosely thrown about, intended more as an insult than anything else. There is a psychiatric diagnosis of narcissistic personality disorder that does exist, but don't be misguided: I am simply saying that as I understand Freud's description of the *id*, the self is the center of self (in my own words). Seriously, out of the eight or so billion people in the world right now, each one of us is focused on ourselves, individually. Of course, it's not a crime to think about yourself, about your needs and desires. It is quite normal. This fundamental truth, if left unidentified and unaddressed, can be a catalyst for following without reason. The reason you put yourself first is instinctual, but I believe that it is something you can address. To do so, you must hone your self-awareness.

Therefore, these two concepts—admitting your following default and getting outside of yourself—are the two most important attributes to exercise to master this instinctual degree. I would like to discuss these two concepts in further detail. Will you follow?

Admit Following Is Your Default

"I y'am what I y'am."
—Popeye

Our human baseline of following is unchangeable and unmovable. We must be aware of it, because if we forget, then simply following will become our master. We are, as a species, lazy thinkers. Psychologists Susan Fiske and Shelley Taylor introduced the concept of the "cognitive miser" in the 1980s (building on work by others before them such as Fritz Heider in the '50s, in a classic example of following).[1] The concept of the cognitive miser is that we only have so much neuro ability, and therefore, we ration it out. We do not *consciously* ration it out. Our brains do it, at a microcellular level behind the scenes, unbeknownst to us.

The rationing out of brain power occurs in the neural synapses and the cerebrospinal fluid between them, which act as superhighways in our brains. This means that our brains lead us by taking the easiest, quickest road in thinking and brain processing. That is the job of the neural synapses and cerebrospinal fluid: not simply to communicate but also to be efficient in doing so, a bit like the map apps we use to help us get from place to place. So, if it is easier and quicker *for your brain* to just go with your instinct and follow, then you will, because that is how your brain naturally works. It is the easiest and most expedient way, and it requires the least amount of brain processing power.

Here's an example. As a teenager, one of the first jobs I ever had was at a garden center. The owner asked me, "What kind of worker do you think is most efficient?" He answered himself, "A short-order cook. He never goes from one side of the kitchen to the other without taking something that needs to go from the first side to the next, or vice versa." Your brain works like a short-order cook, always trying to be as efficient as possible. That is, unless you consciously make it do something different—and you can, because you are a cognitive being.

If you can acknowledge that your baseline exists, you will be able to master that baseline by learning some important skills. Once you have the skills, you can exercise them, employing what I call a *following filter* to proactively address and manage your default baseline. Engaging your following filter requires you to actively force your brain to take the long road when deciding what or who to follow. In this case, you must ask yourself: *I know that I am an instinctual follower. Am I thinking this through or is my miser brain driving me to follow without reason? Am I the master, or the slave? Is my miser brain just being expedient or am I taxing my brain and making it work?*

You must exercise your brain: *brainercise.* Otherwise, you will let your miser brain and your inherent instinct to follow lead you to make some very poor decisions, most likely without even being aware of it. I tell my kids—or anyone who will listen—that they must think of their brain as a muscle. If I told you to drop and give me twenty push-ups, you would likely respond, "No, thank you." Why? Because it is hard. It takes effort. And it is not, necessarily, your idea of fun. Doing it might even hurt. If you really want to see results, it also takes commitment and repetition. No pain, no gain, right? You must sweat. Brainercise is much the same, but with significantly less sweating. Learning new math or science is, literally, hard to do. Learning to be a chess master or a crossword master is hard. But you can choose to learn those things. You can choose to exercise your brain instead of doing things by rote. That exercise is the path to self-awareness.

To remain self-aware and avoid succumbing entirely to my rote, unthinking baseline takes commitment and repetition. I must wake up every morning and acknowledge that I am a follower. Every decision I make must be run through my followship-skills filter to ensure that I am making reasoned decisions. That is, I am not *sequi sin ratione*. I am not *following without reason*. It is interesting to me that from the beginning of recorded history, the masses are led around like sheep, much, if not most, of the time without reason. The rise of the Nazi Party in Germany is the most common example of this mass blindness.

And then there are those who, during such blind devotion, choose otherwise. Dietrich Bonhoeffer, a German theologian and pastor in the early 1900s and outspoken critic of Nazism, wrote on many subjects (well worth your time). His conviction to follow with reason put him at odds with Nazism and eventually led to his execution at Flossenbürg, a German concentration camp, in 1945. Bonhoeffer is a great example of how following is more than learning. He grew frustrated with the blind devotion to unreasoned propaganda that he saw around him. A lot of smart and educated people followed Hitler. Bonhoeffer recognized the pattern of their lack of reason and wrote: "Stupidity is a more dangerous enemy of the good than malice," and "Never again shall we try to persuade the stupid person with reasons, for it is senseless and dangerous."[2]

I am not saying that most people are stupid; I think it is just easier to fall into a habit of mental laziness. Remember the idea of a cognitive miser? Laziness is easy and expedient in terms of brainpower and utilization, and in the back of your brain, that miserly cognition has determined that it is safe to follow, especially at this earliest, instinctual stage of development. Add to that the inclination to follow the leader and we will have come to realize the famous quote from the fictitious, cantankerous, and self-absorbed Horace Vandergelder in the musical film *Hello, Dolly!*: "Ninety percent of the people in the world are fools and the rest of us are in great danger of contamination!"[3] All good humor has an element of truth to it.

Even with a predisposition to mental efficiency that borders on laziness, there still exists the capacity to rationally follow. Reason first, then follow. But the desire to be careful and rational can also drive some people to confuse "anti-following," or nonconformity, with rationality. They will mistakenly say, "I do not follow; therefore, I am rational." This dichotomy of act first, then reason second reverses the process. Often, those who take this path do not see that they are simply following something else. Not following for its own sake is irrational, at times relying on confirmation bias. Such nonconformists do not realize that they are conforming to something else instead, likely without thorough reasoning.

Nevertheless, unlike Bonhoeffer, I *do* believe that we can overcome this hurdle with reason and patience. The first step to mastering that instinct is to *admit* that you have it, that you are *a born follower*. At the very least, to do so will assure that your antennae are up, and you will question yourself, your motives, and your process—and you will do so continually. Then you will have taken your first step toward following with reason.

It Is Not All About You

One of our biggest obstacles to following with reason is our natural self-centeredness. I remember once, when I was young, trying to convince my dad to let me help him work on the car. My dad was not much of a "kid" guy; he was from the school of "children should be seen, not heard." Fully embracing my role as the annoying child, I pestered him into submission. He was working in the garage and the lighting was not the best, so he allowed me to hold the flashlight. It was not more than five seconds before he began yelling at me for not holding the flashlight correctly, then sent me on my way. He fired me, so to speak. The problem was that I was holding the flashlight so *I* could see, not so that *he* could see. I didn't recognize my place in the operation at hand. I didn't do my job. Even after receiving instruction on how to hold the light correctly so he could see, I didn't get it. I wanted to see what was going on! I wanted to have control! It was all about me. Well, he didn't know it at the time, but that experience taught me several valuable lessons, one of which is that it's not all about me.

To give my dad some credit for the practical lesson of holding the flashlight correctly, many years later, when I was an aircraft electrician in the navy, I was working on the flight line in the middle of the night with a senior petty officer. I was in VRC-40, a support squadron at the Naval Air Station in Norfolk, Virginia, where the hangars are right up near the waterfront. The cold wind was blowing strongly from the northeast; engines were revving all around us. And there we were, standing on our shared ladder wearing our cranials (what we called the helmet-like things with built-in goggles and ear protection). It was dark and loud. The flight line is a very dangerous place to be, especially at night and especially during flight operations.

At that point in my life, under those circumstances, do you think I was still holding the flashlight so I could see? No way! You had better believe that I was holding the flashlight so that *he* could see, complete the job, and let us get the hell out of there in one piece! I was laser focused on him, his eyes, and his hands. I zoned out all the distractions and fear and watched his every move, even trying to read his lips in case he gave me instructions that I couldn't hear. Now, I could choose to follow his instructions or my own desires instead. After all, not only was it dangerous out there, but it was freezing cold, and the shop was warm and the coffee there was hot. I chose, through reason, to follow him and his instructions. Not only because it was my job, although that is a well-reasoned conclusion, but also because it was safer to be with him, the experienced man. It was safer for both of us—even the entire flight line. If I had left and run across the flight line, I would have endangered many people, not just myself. I would have been selfish and reckless.

You are not going to follow well (skillfully and with reason) if you are consumed with yourself. I would say that this simple, well-used, universal, and unbiased life lesson is an appropriate second step to temper the instinctual degree of followship. Do you remember Freud's psychoanalytic theory of the *id*, representing our primitive and instinctual desires? At this point in our natural development, we are immature in our attachments because our instinct says "self-first." You are not going to follow well without recognizing this back-of-the-brain driver and disciplining it. There is a reason, if you are familiar with the Bible, that it is written: "Love others as you love yourself." It is because our default is self-love. Not amorous love, of course. But recognize that your instinct is to take care of what you love, and as a result you will always be driven to take the best care of yourself.

"But," you might ask, "doesn't thinking of myself first lead me to safety?" Well, yes. It is clear that self-preservation is instinctual. It hinges on safety. Safety also includes strength in numbers. Humans naturally fear being alone because, historically, being alone is unsafe. The earliest humans even built temples to the gods. Why? For communication? Because they didn't want to be alone? Perhaps, even then, they were doing what came instinctually: following their gods for safety. Nevertheless, we are drawn to safety (putting ourselves first), which draws us to be part of a group. But at the root of the instinctual drive to put ourselves first (safety) lies fear.

The problem is that fear is cunning and devious, and fear can be a liar. As a simple example, I was afraid of swallowing pills for the longest time (embarrassingly, into my early twenties!). As a more complex example, Hitler taught his followers to fear Jews. He created a false truth utilizing irrational, unreasoned fear as a tool. Hopefully, though, as we mature, we become better than our instinctual selves, at least in some respects, and we learn that it is good to master our fear—to not let fear drive our choices without putting some work into the impetus and legitimacy of that fear.

I am talking about fear as it relates to influencing our

following. This can be reasoned or unreasoned fear. I am *not* referring to the fear you might have of a wild animal that is ready to pounce on you. That would be *reasoned* fear. It is rational to be afraid of a wild animal that is ready to kill you. A reasoned reaction would be to run away. I am largely speaking of fear that we are *aware* of when determining what or who to follow and the process of determining whether it is a rational/reasoned fear or if it is an irrational/unreasoned fear.

Plenty of people in our lives—political leaders or your boss or even a "friend," for example—use fear as a tactic to entice people to follow. Did you parents ever say to you, "Do what I told you to do, or else!?" So, our friends and enemies, even our heroes, use fear to get us to follow. Why? Because they want to be followed. They pick an enemy, put a label on them, blame them, and teach you to fear them. During World War II, for example, our own propaganda portrayed our enemies (the Japanese) as less than human just as Hitler's propaganda portrayed the Jews as subhuman.[4] This tactic unites a group. As an aside, you really have to ask yourself: Is it the person in charge in these scenarios who is leading? Or is it the people following that make the leaders "leaders" at all, especially when they do so without reason? Either way, fear is the driver, and fear is used as a tool to manipulate people into following without reason. To reason out the answer, you must reason out the fear. And the only way to reason out the fear is to take yourself out of the equation through self-awareness and intentional cognitive effort.

Therefore, whenever you follow (which you will instinctually do because it's your baseline), you should perform a conscious self-review to cut through the noise. Clarify what, when, who, and how you are following, without including your need for safety in the equation. Take yourself out of the group and review. Essentially, you must look at the decision without listening to your fear. Take yourself, your need for safety, your need to have a sense of belonging—in a word, your *id*—out of the equation. You must ask yourself: *Is my choice-making being skewed by my own drive for self-preservation? By self-love? By fear? By my fear of being left out of the group?* And *What, if anything, am I afraid of? Why am I afraid? Am I afraid to be wrong and ostracized? Am I afraid of change?* You must eliminate fear as an influencer in your reasoned following, and the surest path to that state of mind is first understanding that it is not all about you.

TAKEAWAYS

- We are born followers and will be followers for life. **Following is our baseline**—one that we must admit to as the first step to mastery.

- We, as a species, are lazy thinkers, also known as **cognitive misers**. We only have so much neuro ability

INSTINCTUAL

and, therefore, our brains unconsciously ration it out at a microcellular level—behind the scenes, unbeknownst to us, to conserve brain energy. If our behind-the-scenes brain thinks **it is simply more energy efficient to follow, then it will tell us to do so.**

- **We must exercise our brains:** *brainercise.* Otherwise, we will let our miser brain machine and this inherent instinct to follow lead us to make some very poor decisions, most likely without even being aware of it.

- Don't fall into the trap of "I do not follow; therefore, I am rational." **Not following for the sake of not following is not rational.** Reason first.

- Ignore the *id* (self first). **You are not going to follow well—skillfully and with reason—if you are consumed with yourself.**

- **Fear can be a liar. There is reasoned and unreasoned fear.** Be careful to not fall into the trap of following due to unreasoned fear.

- In order to reason out the answer on what or who to follow, you must reason out the fear, and the surest path to reasoning out the fear is to take yourself out of the equation; **it is not all about you.**

3

INFORMED

The second level of followship is the "informed" degree. At this point, your understanding largely comes from external influences, such as parents, relatives, and broader institutions like schools, churches, and social groups. This stage introduces a new dimension: *how* to follow. Here, the environment you grow up in teaches you that following is not only necessary, but inherently good—no questions asked.

Regardless of whether you develop good followship *skills* during the instinctual degree, you still follow. Even if you haven't reached your full potential, you're always growing and learning. Our innate drive must be turned into disciplined practice—deliberate, refined, and actively developed, like any other skills. Unfortunately, society often conditions us to do the opposite.

During those first several years of our lives, our brains are like soft clay being molded. Well into our twenties, the prefrontal cortex of the frontal lobe is still developing. This area of the brain is responsible for our high-level executive functions, such as reason and judgment.[1] Taken all together, you can see that once you are in a group—be it a family, a club, a school, a company, a political party—you are in a following mode; reason has a way of falling by the wayside. And this part of the equation, this "reason falling by the wayside," *is taught to us*—molded into our neurological pathways.

Take school, for example. From day one, you are placed in a room with kids of roughly the same age, socioeconomic status, and background, and you're addressed as a single unit. You are shaped into a uniform mass of young bodies and minds, following a shared schedule—lining up, attending class, reading, eating, and maybe even napping together. And you loved it! Thank God for recess, right? But even during that seemingly unstructured time, you likely found yourself imitating order, naturally doing what your peers did. Games had rules and play still required structure. Teachers worried if little Charlie or Sarah was off by themselves, assuming it was wrong. This example, though simple, shows how *our society institutionally reinforces following without reason.*

There is a purpose for this type of mandated following, of

course, even though in the process it circumvents individual reasoning. Having our kids obey "because I said so" helps us develop a stable and orderly society. It aids in protection from elements and enemies, in obtaining shelter and food, in order and justice. At the same time, we teach our children to follow without reason. For example, I remember my sister telling me, "They are always watching," referring to the children who kept an eye on my dad and me as we loaded an ice chest with beer for a family gathering and my dad was ordering them to leave us alone.

In a more anthropological example, it is well known that this idea that "the children are always watching us" is how prejudices are handed down from generation to generation. Children are taught by their parents, extended family, and community how the order of society is structured and where they fall within it. Children are taught, in some cases, that other people are not equal to them in one way or another. It wasn't that long ago that this lack of reasoning was evident in the persecution of Jewish people, Indigenous Americans, Aboriginal Australians, and other minority groups. Sadly, this still occurs throughout the world today. Young children will blindly follow. They do not reason that they are blind, because they are *taught* to follow without reason, and they receive positive feedback from this blind obedience. The adults in the room, theoretically, have reasoned this is how one makes an orderly, structured society. But the children only follow—they haven't reasoned anything except one thing—that doing so is good.

As adults, we often return to the informed stage, realizing that—if left unchecked—it reinforces the instinct degree. The lessons learned here shape not only the order of society but also how people reason—or fail to reason—and how they act as a result. So, how do we begin to discipline our followship skills considering this understanding?

Educating Ourselves After the Fact

The second-best way is what I hope to do with this book: help others educate themselves retroactively. The best way would be to advocate a curriculum beginning at the middle school level that would enlighten children of their need to develop a personal discipline to follow with reason. I don't mean telling children what is right and wrong according to society's moral determinations, but explicitly teaching them how the process of reasoning works. That way, in addition to teaching the role of following for a society to function properly, we would also teach the *thought process* of doing so with reason.

In a sense, I am advocating for teaching the principles of *stoicism*—the virtue of reasoning behind decisions or rules. This means shifting the focus from blindly following rules to seeking the reasoning behind them; for instance, prioritizing the search for understanding over merely adhering to the rule itself.

In 2020, at the Business 20 Summit held before the G20 Summit, Vatican News reported comments by Elon Musk on this topic: "Mr. Musk stressed the importance of establishing the relevance of what we learn instead of just learning as a mental obstacle course. He said that critical thinking must be taught early in education as it helps to create some sort of 'firewall' against false concepts."[2] Isn't this exactly what we are discussing? If we were all taught how to approach problem-solving and critical thinking from an early age, we wouldn't have to engage in the "rewiring" process we are now exploring in this book. Mastering this approach early would help counter our instinct for self-preservation (self-love), which often leads to following without reason.

It is not too early to begin teaching philosophy in middle school. What we do teach children at that age, however, is debate (argument). Debate is not about reason, contrary to popular belief. It is about defending a position by utilizing and framing data or evidence to support a position. You are taught to use statistics or economic data, as an example, to come to definitive conclusions when others of equal qualifications and armed with the exact same information will come to a completely different conclusion. No disrespect intended toward those professionals in statistics or economics; they just happen to be easy targets. But if you have ever been in a debate club, or even in an English class having to write a persuasive paper, you are instructed to pick a side and defend it. It has nothing to do with finding truth or finding good or virtue, and it is certainly not about negotiation nor finding common ground.

So, where do we teach that in school? I'm talking about middle and high school, of course. Again, I say it is not too early. When I was in middle school, I was taught that communism was bad, even evil. A sin. I was told it was an honor to sacrifice your life trying to wipe it off the face of the earth. I was never taught *why*, yet I accepted it without question because I had been taught to follow without reason. One day, a kid in high school called me a capitalist. Would you believe I didn't fully understand what that meant? I was even offended! Nevertheless, what we have been taught about following at this stage is that we do it, then build a case around why we do it. That is putting the cart before the horse and is absolutely *not* reasoned following.

Since, clearly, the educational system can't be amended overnight, we must attack this developmental stage of followship retroactively. Remember, this stage is called "informed" for a reason: Our youthful brain was still developing and the roads (neuropathways) of our thoughts and reasoning (or lack thereof) were laid down, never to be revisited again. Until now. Here, in our adult lives, we will repair them or reroute them. For the purposes of this book, I have boiled the work to be done into two action items: 1) pay attention and 2) ask questions. It sounds simple enough, but our world does its level best to take those tools away from us.

Pay Attention

"Whoever has ears ought to hear."
—Matthew 11:15 (ESV)

Pay attention: two eyes, two ears, *one* mouth. It is a colloquial, and sometimes passive-aggressive, way of saying, "Shut up and pay attention." It seems that people have known for a long time that the act of paying attention is important. About 500 years before Christ, the Chinese philosopher Confucius reportedly said, "Keep it simple and focus on what matters." Before him, it is said that Lao Tzu wrote, "Take time to listen to what is said without words." The Bible is full of commentary on the importance of listening and paying attention to details. Jesus is quoted as saying, "A person who has ears ought to hear," and, "A person who is trustworthy in very small matters is also trustworthy in great ones." Even Charles Darwin wrote, in *The*

Descent of Man, "Hardly any faculty is more important for the intellectual progress of man than attention."

In fact, a culture of attention is ingrained in all branches of the military because a lack of attention to detail can cost people their lives. When I was in the navy, at the end of every shift we went through a process to account for every single tool, part, auxiliary part, and piece of supplemental material. A missing wrench could halt operations. There is an acronym, FOD, meaning, "foreign object debris" (or sometimes "damage"). This acronym is utilized in all military branches, but I am most familiar with the air wing of the navy, where sailors would stand side by side, shoulder to shoulder, across the width of the flight line and walk the length of it, looking for FOD—anything on the ground that didn't belong there—knowing that the smallest of objects could be sucked up into a jet engine or hurled like a bullet in the jet blast. Details matter, and detail requires focused attention. Without attention, we will follow without reason. This is the obvious part. But there is science behind this theory as well.

Over the last several decades, more and more brain research— cognitive and molecular neuroscience in particular—has discovered that this attention to detail is significant. Attention is very important and has real impact on our potential brainpower and productivity and is even being studied within the realm of artificial intelligence.[3]

What happens in the brain when you pay attention? Most of us think that *attention* simply means to *focus* on a particular item or task. It does, of course, but that is only the tip of the iceberg. This act of paying attention creates a great deal of brain activity that happens behind the scenes, unbeknownst to us. When we pay attention, neuron activity changes based upon *what* we are focusing on and upon *how much* we are focused. The neuron activity can increase or decrease. This activity is building, strengthening, rerouting neural pathways—pathways that may be utilized for reasons other than the particular item or task you are currently focusing on. It is the cholinergic system in the brain that is responsible for stimulating these neurons to increase by transmitting acetylcholine.[4] But increase is not all. Recently, in September of 2023, the Nanyang Technological University in Singapore published findings suggesting that in addition to acetylcholine, there is another neurotransmitter, gamma-aminobutyric acid (GABA), which is also in the attention game. But in this case, its role is to inhibit neurons from receiving and sending messages. Thus, we have both an increase and a decrease. Furthermore, there is also some fascinating work done in research on mirror neurons, which are responsible for doing exactly what the name implies: mirroring (mimicking/following) what we observe.[5]

All this activity going on behind the scenes in your brain

happens when you focus and pay attention. This chemical activity is directed and has a purpose. In other words, your brain is reacting based on what you think is important and worthy of your attention. Not surprisingly, you can make your brain get better at paying attention by exercising attention: brainercise. Essentially, you make your brain faster and stronger. Yes, you can exercise your nervous system. Those neurons will grow or shrink based on *how much* you exercise them. Paying attention is exercise. That's why it is "hard" to study. Think of your muscles when you exercise, or when you don't. To sharpen your followship skills, you must exercise by paying attention.

In my flashlight story, would you say I was paying attention to my father? No. I was only concerned with myself, and as a result, I was not paying attention, even after my dad clarified his instructions. While it would be easier to go about our day not worrying about this "following baseline," if you're going to follow anyway, why not do it well? Without discipline, we fall prey to the many predators who want to take advantage of our lazy, unbrainercised minds. They don't call themselves *predators*, of course. They may not consciously know about your baseline drive to follow, either. Some do, and they use it as a tool or even a weapon of manipulation.

I worked for a company once where the CEO openly used "groupthink" as a management tool. He knew it and used it.

He threatened or got rid of anyone who was not on board. Undoubtedly, he learned this method by following, reading, and watching others who had "success" utilizing this dubious method. These people are in the business of influencing and taking advantage of people. They may disguise their efforts or even delude themselves into thinking that their actions are for the benefit of the organization, but I believe that if you peel back the onion, their actions come from self-preservation. You must pay attention in order to protect yourself, to control your baseline, and to control your propensity to follow these influencers.

Brainercise: How to Exercise Paying Attention

- **Be still.** "All of humanity's problems stem from man's inability to sit quietly in a room alone," said Blaise Pascal, a seventeenth-century Frenchman who was a child prodigy on a range of subjects from math to philosophy.[6] While this isn't meant to be a religious book, religion has some very good life instructions. I'd be willing to bet that all forms of spirituality advocate the act of being still. I'm pretty sure everyone prays and has prayed since the beginning of time. I recommend several times a day finding a place to be alone and silent, without doing a thing—five to ten minutes at a time, minimum. In resting your senses, I believe you give your mind a rest.

- One of the big lessons in weight lifting and bodybuilding is when to stop lifting weights and give your body a chance to recover. The same goes for your brain. Being still means no stimulus—preferably dark, absolutely no sound, and you might think it goes without saying, but no self-inflicted electrical shock! There was a study reported in the journal *Science*, in 2014, of an experiment at the University of Virginia in Charlottesville where subjects chose to shock themselves while they were tasked to sit alone in a room for fifteen minutes with no other stimulus other than their own thoughts. So, 67 percent of men and 25 percent of women chose to shock themselves.[7]

- **No multitasking.** Please, please, please, do not multitask. It's essentially akin to teaching yourself bad habits. I'm not talking about running the dishwasher while you fold clothes or watering the garden while you are mowing that backyard. I'm talking about splitting your immediate attention between two things. For example, when I try to listen to and grasp what is being said on a radio talk show while trying to formulate an idea of my own and write it down. Not only do I fail at both tasks in this example, but I am also teaching my brain how to operate suboptimally. It is true. Just like you can exercise your brain by paying attention, the inverse applies as well. Don't teach your brain bad habits.

- **Play music.** Learn to play some musical instrument or, barring that, play some mental games such as Sudoku. It is true what you have read about the benefits of this type of brain exercise. These activities require your attention. They are good brain exercises.

- **Exercise your other senses.** Sight, hearing, touch, and even smell and taste require exercise as well. I have no basis for this assertion other than it makes a logical kind of sense to me that involving and exercising your senses will exercise the entire brain system, thereby enhancing your ability to pay attention. Back when I would put my young daughter to bed, after I tucked her in and we said our prayers, I would lie on the floor in her room and put on a song ("The Divine Mercy Chaplet"—it's like a chant). I would lower the volume to the point where we couldn't hear it. Then we would lie there in the silence, nothing to hear except the ringing in our ears. Soon, there were other sounds we could distinguish. After about five or ten minutes, we could start hearing the music. Pretty cool, right? Our ears adjusted to the silence like our eyes adjusted to the darkness.

- **Practice awareness.** If you find yourself trying to pay attention and then find you are not focused, I think that is a good sign. To me, it means that you are aware of your drift. You should listen to your brain. Be aware of how it is working and responding to the effort. Take it as a sign to take a break. Get some air, take a walk, do another task for a while. Perhaps a short nap. But come back to it, eventually. Then start over. And over. And over. And over. It's called exercise.

Ask Questions

"Why?" is the favorite question of every two-to-five-year-old and the most frustrating question directed to every parent. It's also probably the most important question you will ever ask. It is a simple way to see what separates you from other living beings. You can ask "Why?" And you can answer! Interestingly, this is where followship gets complicated, because not only are there educational and hierarchal aspects involved, but there is free will. "Put your coat on," I might tell my child. "Why?" they ask. I respond, "Because it's cold outside." "Why is it cold, Daddy?" "Well, it's the season. It's winter." They respond,

"What is winter?" Back and forth it goes, and now you know that this could go on forever. "Just put your coat on!" "*But why?!*" "Because I said so!" It can be so frustrating. On one hand, everyone wants their children to grow up asking why, but on the other hand, maybe not *right now*. We want to say, "Hold that thought and let me get back with you when you are older and can understand. But don't stop asking why!" It's complicated.

Believe it or not, there is a lot of stuff to unpack here. A child has the instinct to follow orders because they are born that way, and they have found that their parent provides food, shelter, safety, and affection. The child has also been taught by their parent to follow (or else!). It's an instinct that is now mandated and reinforced. Put another way, the child has become self-aware, albeit still developing, and so there is the drive to obtain knowledge and understanding, an *instinctual curiosity*. Then comes the quashing of that curiosity. They have a reinforced instinct, but they want to know things (the "why") that may conflict with the first two objectives (instinctual and informed). The querying is quashed by their instinctual drive in the first place and by the mandated instructions of their parents. If it sounds like a circular formula, that's because it is. It is good to want to understand. It is good to ask questions. It is also good to know when to *stop* asking questions and *start* following orders.

So, we teach our children to follow without reason. But we must have order in our families and in society; therefore, it seems there is no other way. The consequence that we unknowingly inflict is a reinforcement of the instinct to follow, *sequi sin ratione*. The only option I see to rectify the situation is to do what we are doing here: revisit the conversation as adults when we can reteach ourselves to reason well, even when dealing with authority. Don't stop asking *yourself* questions. After all, what is "reason" anyway? Reason is not a destination; reason is a *process*. An internal, hopefully cyclical, process—one that you repeat in your mind over and over again, even about the same or similar subjects, and especially regarding following.

As an adult, you will find that questions are good, but you can answer most yourself with a little effort. Carl Jung, the Swiss psychiatrist, psychoanalyst, and founder of analytical psychology said, "To ask the right question is already half the solution of a problem."[8] Add to that asking the right *person*, and you are almost there. So, by process of elimination, start with yourself. Drive yourself to find the answer.

Professors often tell their students, "There are no bad questions." But we can ask them at the wrong time or in the wrong way. I remember an experience when I was working my first professional job. By "professional," I mean I worked in an office as a paid intern. I received an assignment, with very little guidance, to compile a report for legal and litigation expenses. I put the report together, added some analytics, a cover page, table of contents, and a summary. I had gone above and beyond, and I was very proud of the final product. When the CFO of the company reviewed my work, I could see in his eyes and hear it in his voice that he was impressed. I was so proud of myself, thinking that I'd made such a good impression. Then, he asked me to reprint it because the ink was not *dark* enough. I asked him—remember, this man was the CFO—how to change the ribbon on the printer. Not a good question. I could see him deflate like a balloon. The light came out of his eyes, and he was clearly bothered by my question. He said in a gruff voice, "I'll change it." Realizing my error, I tried to backtrack and say that I was sorry, I'd handle it. But the admiration I'd gained with the quality of the report had been lost in one poorly thought-out question. I should have asked myself and found the answer on my own. I was lazy and didn't want to exercise my brain. Having said that, I don't mean to dissuade anyone from asking for help. Elite followers always ask questions, and they always ask for help. The difference is that they will have mastered the wisdom of knowing *when* to do so. And they will always start with themselves.

I am not simply referring to the "why" question. I am including all types of questions. Simon Sinek's popular book *Start with Why* focuses on the emotional, internal aspect of asking questions and searching for answers—at least, that is my take on his approach. I recommend the book, but my approach is more directed to reason. Reason over emotion. It's about searching for and understanding the conclusions you reach through rational thought processes. Not just "why?" but "to what end?"

One way of understanding our conclusions is wrapped up in the old expression "question authority." While that's valuable advice, I believe the authority you should question most often is yourself. How else can you follow with reason? Of course, questioning yourself requires caution. There is a science to consider here, as with everything else we have discussed to this point. There is a reason that leading questions are not allowed in the courtroom. And there are other effective ways of manipulating the brain into a train of thought that leads to a desired conclusion. The most effective salespeople are masters at invoking thoughts and desires in our minds.

Here are some practices I have incorporated when asking questions on my journey to follow with reason:

1. **Be clear.** The first task in asking or answering an intelligent question is to ensure the playing field is level. Even if you speak the same language as the person you are asking the question of, semantics matter. For example, we cannot

talk about whether multitasking is good or bad without first agreeing on what multitasking *is*, followed by what we mean by *good* (and *bad*). Vagueness and ambiguity are killers of clear communication.

- **Keep things open-ended.** Don't use rhetorical or leading questions. Stick to questions that can draw out a broad range of answers from another person. Examples of open-ended questions include: What do you think about what I just said? How does that work? Why did you choose that option? When will the project be complete? But, "You didn't really mean that, did you?" is a leading question. Which reminds me, stay away from "you" statements. An example of a rhetorical question is, "Are you really going to wear that?" when the person you're speaking to is clearly already wearing it.

- **Remember the spectrum.** I have developed some personal mantras, one of which is: There is rarely ever a single answer to something. When listening to answers, remember, rarely is the answer just one thing. What we think of as absolutes are almost never absolute. Everything is on a spectrum.

- **Seek to understand, not compete.** Ask questions to understand, not debate. Good questions are never about winning or losing, but always about understanding. And be careful not to fall into the trap of simple answers merely because the complicated answers tax your brain—some things, maybe even most, are complicated.

- **Be aware of your body.** Our bodies will display signs of irrationality—volume increase in voices, rigidity of posture, gut tensing, nausea, and so on—often long before we're willing to admit to them. If you find yourself feeling any of these ways, refer to the next practice.

- **Put yourself on time-out.** Time-outs are not only okay, they are good. Wait to ask or answer a question. Take time to process the answers.

- **Start with yourself.** Most questions should be directed inward, to yourself. This is pretty important.

I was brought up in a very traditional family. Life was very fixed and regimented. Rules were fundamental. Respect for authority was fundamental. My dad, grandfathers, and all seven uncles served in the military. Then there was church, school, music, and sports . . . all strictly rule-bound. By the time I got to high school, I was up to my neck in this informed degree of followship.

Remember, we start with instinct, then we're informed. Take orders. Do as I say. Follow without reason. So, looking back to my opening story in the book, it is not surprising that I got myself in a terrible and dangerous situation when I was fifteen.

It is heartbreaking to submit to authority to the extent that I did, and after it was over, you didn't hear a peep out of me about it. I'm sixty years old and just now seeing it for what it is and talking about it. Why didn't I pay attention? Why didn't I ask questions? The way I see it now, I was operating exactly as I was taught to operate. In this chapter we've discussed how to address this informed degree of following—how to rewire our brains. It can be done. It just takes some brainercise.

Lastly, in asking questions, don't be surprised when the answers are complicated. Answers may start with, "Well, it depends." Most things are complicated. Yet, much of the time we want simple answers. The simple answers are easier on the brain, right? It's easy to say World War I started because Archduke Franz Ferdinand of Austria was assassinated or that World War II was all Hitler's fault, or that inflation or unemployment or some other economic issue is caused by one policy, or that there is only one way to respond to a pandemic. Don't fall into the trap of settling for the simple answer because it is easy.

TAKEAWAYS

- **The "informed" degree** of followship reinforces the "instinct" degree of followship, using the "instinct" degree as a lever.

- In this "informed" degree, **we are taught to follow first, then build a case to support our reasons for following.** This is backward. This is how biases are handed down and teaches to follow without reason. So, reason first. Then follow.

- We are taught this unreasoned following path in our youth because it is at least partly necessary to establish a functioning society. It would be best to also teach our children philosophy and stoic reasoning at an early age. Barring that, **we must unlearn this unreasoned following path as adults.** Our brains were literally wired to work to follow without reason. It will take work to rewire our brains.

- The field of neuroscience—cognitive and molecular neuroscience in particular—has discovered that **paying attention is very important** (beyond simple focus) and has real impacts on our potential brainpower and productivity and is even being studied within the realm of artificial intelligence.

- **Your brain should be thought of as a muscle.** It can be exercised—brainercised. Paying attention and asking questions, particularly of ourselves, can exercise our neuropathways. Particularly, answering the question, "To what end?" **Beware the simple answer.**

- **Reason is a process, not a destination**—the process never ends.

4

LEARNED

I had just turned thirty and moved to a new state to start a brand-new job. It was a job working for a small company, which meant that I would have the opportunity to get my hands into a variety of aspects of the business. Everyone should work for a small business, especially early in their career. This was my second small company in a row that I had worked for, and I loved it. I was primarily responsible for the accounting and reporting for a major part of the business and, as my father had told me, being in accounting gives you great insight into the workings of the entire organization, not just the finances.

With that in my back pocket, I spent a great deal of "off-duty" time (code for unpaid overtime) developing a monthly report that would convey what I thought were the important data points that leadership should need and want to keep track of. I believed I was shining the flashlight so they could see—even so they could see things they didn't know, things they didn't realize they needed to see in the first place. I started putting the report out monthly. It took some effort to produce it, but after about nine months of not hearing anything about it, I just stopped.

A few months later, I was reprimanded for having stopped the reporting. Ha! My boss told me that the owner of the company had said, "How can I steer this business without this report?" I started the reporting up again, but now I had a title: "The Helm." I even put a picture of a ship's helm on it. The owner signed one for me with a simple "Thanks" on it. I have that copy still, to this day. It is a story I have gone on to use with people who have worked for me to demonstrate that even when you don't know it, people are following you, what you say, and what you do. Remember that you steer the ship from behind. Like my dad taught me with the flashlight, be sure to shine your light in the right places so the right people can see. Thanks, Dad.

Learned Following

This leads us to the next degree of followship: "learned." We are now at the level where we become aware that we can learn. This is the point where skillful followers are maturing, knowingly or unknowingly. Importantly, society doesn't call them *followers*, though. These are young adults who appear successful by societal standards. They continue to grow in mastering the skill set that we are bringing to light here, which leads to further success in future leadership roles.

On the other hand, those unskilled in this work who appear successful by traditional standards are also placed in leadership roles, yet they go on to struggle with being effective leaders. The latter group let the first two degrees of followership development take up permanent residence in their psyche. Folks in this category are more interested in authority, control, prestige, and their career. They believe, partly because they were taught this, that they "learned" how to follow, and now they can put all of that behind them because they have graduated to being "a leader." Too bad, for everyone. They may have gotten into a leadership position because they were at the right place at the right time, they were the only option or the least-bad option, they took instruction well, maybe they were technically astute, but it stops there. You never hear, "We promoted them into a leadership role because of their followership skills." At least, not yet.

The world knows we need better leaders—or better people in leadership roles. That's why, as I pointed out at the beginning of the book, so much money is spent trying to develop leaders. But this leadership-development complex has it all wrong. We don't need better leaders in leadership roles, we need *skilled followers* in leadership roles. People who *sequi cum ratione*. It's more than just learning, creating, or even decision-making. Following with reason means becoming intimately involved with the process of reasoning and responding to your environment. This is the process by which you obtain, filter, store, and react to data— resulting in reasoned following.

Have you heard the axiom, "The best defense is a good offense"? This applies to following with reason because both describe being proactive in an environment where you are being attacked rather than simply being reactive to the attack. I believe that expression may come close to what I am trying to describe. We are attacked, so to speak, by our instinctual desire, which is further complicated by our environment (external and internal). Our strategic defense is to develop a process of how we use reason in our choices—disciplined followership skills. First, we admit we are followers. Second, we admit that it is not all about us, taking ourselves out of the equation. Third, we pay attention to details. Fourth, we ask well-thought-out questions, especially to ourselves. And now we start getting answers and are faced with identifying false influences or influencers, the false truth that comes from "hyperstimuli."

Hyperstimuli are data points that have made it through to this point in our environment, either by design or by ancillary means. It could be anything from back-of-the-brain impulses, such as fatigue or hunger; right-brained (emotional) issues, such as fear, anger, envy, or other emotional baggage; or left-brained (logical) concepts coming in the form of "aerosol data" or "noise" that can come in volume or breadth, loudly (obviously and repeatedly) or silently (stealthily)—both are, essentially, an overabundance of data.

For example, I know people who love to have their TVs on all the time, even if they are not in the room. It is tuned to some news station, but it could be anything. They aren't really listening, but they are on some level because you cannot turn off your ears. This is a simple example of noise. If, on the other hand, you are watching with interest, aerosol data includes the side stories in the news, commentary on the events when you just want facts, or even commercials. This concept can apply to the workplace, your church, the mall, on vacations, and essentially everywhere, all the time. All these things affect the process of determining who or what we decide to follow. In a word, they are distractions.

Most distractions—perhaps more than half—are easy to identify. These are the distractions that are clearly unrelated to the task at hand. However, it is still necessary to consciously go through the mental process of identifying and eliminating them, lest they slip by and affect your following path.

Start by making a list of distractions that you have identified in your own life. Then create a separate list of relevant inputs, divided into two categories: variable and fixed. Variable inputs include factors like the time of day, your physical and mental state (whether you're tired, unwell, or feeling great), the person you're interacting with, the reason for the interaction, and the location. Fixed inputs might include things like your job responsibilities or even your birth order.

Believe it or not, these factors will all impact your reasoning. This is why I emphasize that following is a process, much like trying to hit a moving target. Thus, the need to recognize and handle these factors accordingly. You might find it helpful to categorize them, then systematically eliminate distractions and focus on what is truly relevant.

Second, focus on the distractions we are typically blinded to. Each of us has our own "push-button" issues that influence our ability to follow with reason. These issues could be certain emotions, such as pride or fear, coming from the right side of your brain, or they might be compulsiveness or overanalysis—from the left side of your brain. Maybe they are fatigue, dehydration, or hunger, which originate in the root of the brain.

In the diagram that follows, the idea of the "filters" demonstrates how we might recognize and eliminate distractions. The filters are questions—attentive, well-thought-out questions, mostly directed at yourself regarding the information coming from each of the spheres of influence at work on you at any given time. The process is deconstructing and reconstructing information after filtration.

Using myself as an example, let's start with the left (logical) side of the brain: I am researching a particular topic looking for a specific answer. I am reading and find something interesting but unrelated. Do I follow it? No. Well, I shouldn't, at least not right now. My filter says write it down (deconstruction) and take it up later. How about the root of the brain? The obvious one is the alcoholism (master distractor), but let's go with fatigue—I am tired. The deconstructing (filtering) can be simply acknowledging the fatigue and its impact on my work, and the reconstructing can be resting or writing a note to revisit my work product later. Not filtering would be to ignore its impact, thinking my work is fine. And it could indeed be fine, but it is certainly not my *best*.

Moving to the right (emotional) side of the brain, this side wants to be correct. Deconstruction says to acknowledge (filter) that impulse and reconstruct an unemotional analysis. Remember, our baseline is to follow. We are aiming to do so *with reason* that we base on filtered information, including the various hyperstimuli.

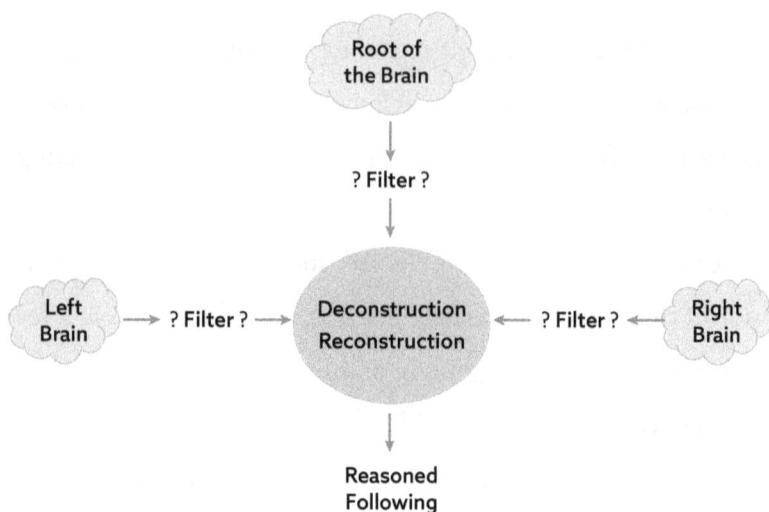

Figure 4.1

Identify and Isolate Distractions

Have you ever been in the car with your spouse trying to decide where to go eat? "Where do you want to go?" "I don't know. Where do *you* want to go?" "I don't care. Where do *you* want to go?" *Oy!* Then you end up arguing about who was the last person to decide where to go eat. You are both completely derailed and unfocused on the original decision, which was where to eat. Why? Because of the distractions: the noise or ancillary things going on behind the scenes in your brain. In the root of the brain, you have hunger and maybe even fatigue. Being "hangry" is a real, quantifiable thing.[1] When you are hungry, your brain knows it. Your blood sugar is low, and your body releases cortisol and adrenaline in response. These chemicals stimulate neurons that block your ability to reason. Your brain now wants you to focus on your hunger and to be aggressive enough to get some food.[2]

But that's not all your brain wants. In your right brain, the emotional side, you want to win or be right (same thing).[3] Winning feels good and being right releases all sorts of happy chemicals: endorphins, serotonin, dopamine, and oxytocin. Your brain knows this and, as with any addictive behavior, it seeks to obtain and repeat whatever brought about this happy feeling. So, being right is addictive.

And what about your left brain? Your logical side is leafing through the calendar in your mind, reviewing the last few places you've gone to eat and who made that decision. Now your hearing is gone, and your speech is on remote control because your mind is busy with the calendar. It is such a cluster of competing activity! This scenario plays out in all sorts of arguments, discussions, and debates where the aerosol data distracts us from the point at hand. What were we talking about anyway? Oh yeah—where do we go eat? There are so many things distracting our reason or competing with our desire to follow.

Some of those distractions are within us and others outside of us. While psychologists Susan Fiske and Shelley Taylor introduced the concept of the "cognitive miser" in the

1980s, behavioral economist and Nobel Prize winner Daniel Kahneman and his team have researched decision-making theory and the breakdowns within it. Most recently, in his book *Noise*, Kahneman explains how distractions and biases impact our decision-making, resulting in errors and less-than-optimum results.[4] These and other studies of heuristics and cognitive bias are not new. They all seek to describe the human drive to simplify our decision-making process and how we accomplish this simplification. The research led me to believe that our instinct is subject to cognitive bias, and therefore a potential distraction from reasoned following. A distraction that needs to be addressed, and the place to begin is the inputs.

The Illusion of Independence in Followship

Recall that at this learned stage, many of us believe we've outgrown the need to follow. As adults—now educated and experienced—we see ourselves as leaders. As a result, we often dismiss the idea of examining what or whom we are pursuing. The assumption is, "I don't follow anyone, so there's no need to put effort into this." This mindset is both misleading and dangerous. It affects every aspect of our lives—personal, professional, and communal. We all follow something, whether we realize it or not.

Take today's political news landscape as an example. In a media environment driven by profit, we are often led to follow distractions rather than facts. Sensationalism and noise dominate because they sell. The more sensational the story, the more views, clicks, shares, and comments it generates—and that attention directly translates into advertising dollars and network profits.

In this setting, maybe only 20 percent of the news is relevant, while 80 percent is designed to distract. Whether the information is exaggerated, biased, or misleading doesn't matter—the goal is to capture your attention, not inform you. The result is that we, as consumers, follow the noise. It's crucial to understand that this manipulation affects everyone, regardless of where you fall on the political spectrum. If you believe it doesn't apply to you, then the deception has already worked. The challenge is to break free from this passive following and actively question what you are being led to focus on each time you turn on the news.

Whether we examine distractions in the news or distractions of a personal nature, the Pareto principle applies here, commonly known as the 80/20 rule. The Pareto principle posits 20 percent of the actions in any endeavor produce 80 percent of the results. There is a great deal of noise in that 80 percent, when the most important data is in that 20 percent, even though there is noise there too. I might call the noise in the 20 percent "bleed-over noise." Quite often what we think is in the 20 percent will also contain extreme or amplified pieces of what is in the 80 percent. The amount varies based on the amplification, but we know it is there because to make it into the 20 percent bucket, it must be extremely loud and obvious. Even if we're generous and say that the core information amounts to 10 percent, this means that, in the end, we could be looking at a 90/10 split where only 10 percent of the information, after reasoning out the other 90 percent, is worth our following. We can't just ignore the other 90 percent, though, because there may be some hidden detail in that bulk data that is important to decipher in searching for and finding the answer on who or what to follow. At the same time, what made it to the 20 percent should not be guaranteed and may need to be filtered down to 10 percent. Nothing can be received without a critical mindset.

The phrase *ceteris paribus*—often used in economics—means "all other things being equal or unchanged." For our purposes, the phrase is completely false. In real life, all other things are *never* equal, because they are not equal in importance. We know that the smallest of things can influence a decision. The "noise" in decision-making in one situation may be between 80 percent and 90 percent, while in a completely different situation, the "noise" may only be between 10 percent and 20 percent of "importance." As Kahneman points out, why do people suggest having surgery in the morning versus the afternoon, even if the

same surgeon would be working at each of those times? Because
the surgeon is fresher in the morning. It's funny, but even how
hungry or thirsty you are at a given time could influence a decision. But, if you can get the *process* of decision-making about
what or who to follow to include identifying and removing
distractions, then that is a material achievement.

Take the story where I held the flashlight for my dad. What
was my decision-making process? As a child, I didn't have one,
so I stuck to my instinctual and informed degrees. My instinctual miser brain was in charge, and my informed following
principles were firmly in place. As an adult, now that you know
your default is to follow, what will be your routine, your process
for filtering the noise and evaluating your options with reason?
It doesn't have to be the same process for each decision, but
humans are creatures of habit, and you will likely follow the
same process in evaluating options. How do you tame it?

You can start by adopting a filtering process, one by which
you identify and isolate distractions. Everyone is different, so
this will require some reflection on your part. What distracts
you? Identify it, filter it, and isolate it. This may seem overkill,
frankly, but learning a discipline is tough. It takes practice. This
step is akin to finding the lowest common denominator. Perhaps even a process of elimination. Either way, you won't make
a reasoned decision to follow if you are distracted.

Here are some steps to help identify and eliminate distractions:

2. **Breathe**. Most people are familiar with the metaphor "canary in the coal mine." Believe it or not, up until the 1980s, coal miners used to have canary birds with them in the mines as early detectors of poisonous gasses. Your breathing rate can be your own canary—an early indicator of the presence of a distraction, in particular a right-brain distraction. Your own emotions are a form of distraction from rational following. Irregular breathing can be an indication of euphoria or anxiety, both of which are enemies of rational thought. Practice regulating your breathing, especially during emotional times.

- **Be aware of your environment**: physical, mental, emotional. You may not be able to fully eliminate things in your environment, but being aware of them can help you process or filter them out of your reasoning. Do you have a deadline? Are you alone? Is it night or day, loud or quiet? Are you rested or fatigued? What other stimulus is involved—any drugs or alcohol? All of these are distractions from reasoned following.

- **Identify fixed and variable components**. I pick on *ceteris paribus* a lot, but the idea of it is good; that is, to attempt to create a scientific analysis where the path to reasoning is controlled, as with a controlled experiment.

- **Circle back to your original goal.** Ask yourself if you're being pulled away and, if so, by what? Anything that can be isolated and removed from the equation is a distraction and should be removed from your reasoning. Think of the process of elimination. And circle back to ask, "To what end?"

- **Know your "push buttons."** We are all unique, but we all have them of one sort or another, to one degree or another. What is even worse is that we usually telegraph our push buttons to others. These are distractions that we even use to distract ourselves, even subconsciously, instead of focusing on the issue at hand.

Eliminate Biases

Bias is an obvious component of the distractions block. However, the subject is significant enough to warrant a separate callout. Bias is more than just playing favorites. I first started learning about bias in terms of prejudice in the '70s. I was in a private, Catholic middle school but, interesting to note, I didn't really know that I was doing anything differently than everyone else. I was just going to school. I don't think there was one Black kid in the entire school. Bias and prejudice were not things I really thought about. Given what was going on in the country at the time, it was at least mentioned, and I did grasp it—or at least I thought I did.

I attempted to use the idea of bias and prejudice by blaming my low grade in English class on my white teacher, telling my parents that she was prejudiced against Mexican Americans. The truth is, I really didn't understand the concept. Bias is usually taught in terms of race, gender, and ethnicity, but it is far more than that. Often, we follow bias without reason. Remember, our brains are not fully developed until our late twenties, and during our first several years, our brains are very malleable—like a lump of wet clay. We are taught everything we know.

So, for me, I grew up thinking American-made cars were the best and that Buicks, in particular, were the *best* of the best. In reality, cars made in Japan had better maintenance records and were cheaper. I was taught labor unions were a plague, but I didn't know what a union was, only that I was against them. I also learned that only Catholics went to Heaven, though that is not Catholic doctrine. The Dallas Cowboys were God's gift to the world and the Pittsburgh Steelers were akin to communists. Communists, of course, were just plain *evil*—though I never met one and didn't know an economic model from a hole in the ground. I was a proud Republican, though I didn't know what that meant either! Bias is so ingrained in us that it is part of who we are, and it becomes a component of our value set and idea of justice. And we follow our bias often without reason.

The most successful followers—those who employ reason—learn to work through these challenges internally. The way I see it, the key to eliminating bias is straightforward: you must *want* to do it. I agree that when we are young, our brains are malleable, developing, and shaped by various influences. This concept of neuroplasticity supports the idea that we are born as followers and further molded by our environments.

Certainly, the same applies to bias. We may not be born with biases, but we're certainly taught them during our formative years, when our brains are still wiring themselves. To use a simple metaphor, it's as if the pathways in our brains are being laid down, set, and reinforced, like superhighways. As we grow older, our brains tend to ignore the issue of bias, incorporating it into our thinking without us even realizing it. Bias operates behind the scenes.

Fiske and Taylor's research on cognitive misers explains that our brains prefer the easiest, quickest route when processing information. If following our instincts or biases is the simplest option, that's the path our brains will take because it requires the least mental effort. Bias often goes unchallenged because it's the easier, more automatic response.

This seemingly automatic response means we often think we are "hardwired" when we talk about certain biases, behaviors, and preferences. These traits may be difficult to untangle, but it's not impossible. It boils down to *wanting*. If you want to lose weight or get in shape, you must diet and exercise. Nothing will happen until you change the desire from "I want to lose weight," or "I want to get in shape," to "I want to diet," or "I want to exercise." Do you see how the equation changed? It is a *decision* about what we really want.

This shift in mindset is how you get to the root of bias. You cannot simply say, "I want to *not* be biased." You must decide that you want to drill down to identify the bias and eliminate it. It's a subtle shift from a passive to an active mindset. It goes without saying that you cannot follow with reason most effectively if you are carrying biases, consciously or unconsciously. And it is the unconscious that you really have to worry about. We are all different, so it takes some individual soul-searching and a commitment to do the work.

That is not to say the commitment is simple. Keep in mind that we have an addictive default to want to be right. Being right releases dopamine in the brain, that feel-good, affirmative chemical. This is where the stick-to-itiveness of a bias comes from: a default belief or way of thinking that is so fundamental to your way of thinking that you aren't even conscious it exists.

And it is a self-reinforcing phenomenon. Not good or bad. Not one side or the other. It simply *is*.

The following chart illustrates what I am attempting to define in the form of a bias infinity loop. It is extremely difficult to break out of a bias, even after identifying it, so you must *want* to break the loop. It is a loop because your bias feels good when affirmed, which leads to repeating it. You feel good because when you are affirmed, chemicals are released in your brain and travel down these superhighways that were built in your brain during your youth. On the other hand, if your bias is challenged (again, due to the brain construction that was

Bias Infinity Loop

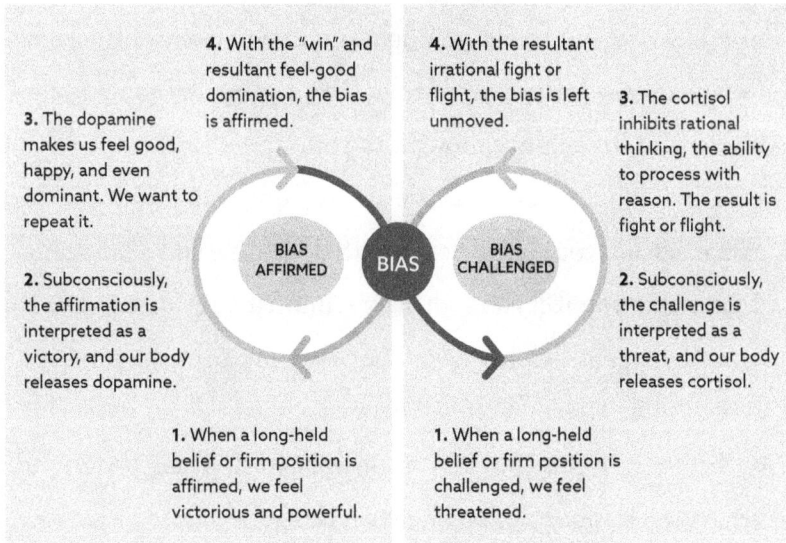

3. The dopamine makes us feel good, happy, and even dominant. We want to repeat it.

2. Subconsciously, the affirmation is interpreted as a victory, and our body releases dopamine.

4. With the "win" and resultant feel-good domination, the bias is affirmed.

1. When a long-held belief or firm position is affirmed, we feel victorious and powerful.

BIAS AFFIRMED — **BIAS** — **BIAS CHALLENGED**

4. With the resultant irrational fight or flight, the bias is left unmoved.

3. The cortisol inhibits rational thinking, the ability to process with reason. The result is fight or flight.

2. Subconsciously, the challenge is interpreted as a threat, and our body releases cortisol.

1. When a long-held belief or firm position is challenged, we feel threatened.

Figure 4.2

done in your youth), your brain releases chemicals that make you feel threatened, angry, irritable—all of which inhibit and even prevent the ability to reason. The only way out of this bias infinity loop is to want to break it. And to break it, you have to want to exercise it out.

When a bias is challenged, all hell breaks loose in your brain chemistry. You can't allow that to happen. It never ceases to amuse me when someone says, "Take the emotion out of the argument" or "You can't have a rational discussion with emotion involved." Emotions are *always* involved. It is part of your being, and you cannot eliminate your emotions. You must master them. Stress, feeling unsafe, mistrust, losing—these things cause your body to release cortisol, which interferes with your ability to reason. So as a result, you fight, or argue a point, or default to your biases for self-protection. This happens automatically, inside your brain, unbeknownst to you.

Then, if you win in whatever situation you're in, even a casual debate, your brain floods with dopamine and adrenaline. That makes you feel good, thereby reinforcing the desire to win again and again—to be right. The best you can do to stop this cycle is to be aware that it will happen and work hard to head it off before it begins. But you must want to stop this pattern of behavior. Only *you* can break that cycle.

So how do we break the cycle? Every situation is different on any given day and in any given moment, because biases are personal. The first step is to admit to our biases or, at least, that they *could be there*. Then educate yourself. If you are making yourself uncomfortable, that is probably a good sign that you are making progress. Honestly, the "wanting" is the hardest part; identifying it is not as difficult. With my alcoholism, the disease is/was not the bias, but it was a major distraction that has taken a lifetime to acknowledge and overcome. The bias was that everyone does it. That's how I grew up. The bias complicated the distraction— an example of the infinity loop. I had to admit it was there and then educate myself. Then I was able to take action to rectify both the bias and the distraction.

Here's another example. My son told me a story about when he was at the Naval Academy. He said that when he was there, they would eat together as a squad or small team. There was a hierarchy at the table, of course. If you were to get in trouble for not following a protocol, then you were ordered to stop eating and sit at attention. From what he told me, you would have to lean over the table at a forty-five-degree angle, still sitting at attention, and they would put a honey bear on the table in front of your face. As you stared into the eyes of the honey bear—which, by itself, is hilarious—everyone at the table would try to make you break, either by humor or insult, or whatever might work. If you broke eye contact with the honey bear or broke any form of attention, then you could not eat. The honey bear was called the "Bearing Bear."

I love the story. It is about exercising your ability to keep your bearing while under stress and distraction, and it fits perfectly with the idea of honing the degree of learned follower. Imagine the amount of self-discipline and mental and emotional strength it takes in that moment. You are tired, hungry, and thirsty. You literally smell the food in front of you and see it in your peripheral vision. You hear everyone eating. In fact, it echoes in the dining hall. Is it so loud, with all sorts of sounds, clanging plates, and ringing voices reverberating off the walls, floor, and ceiling. It is noisy! Is it hot or cold? Am I sitting at attention correctly? Why is that bear staring at me? And at the table, you have direct input—everyone is talking to you—but what do you listen to when there is that one-and-only command you need to hear? Just waiting for the order, you must tell yourself, *Eliminate the distractions! Filter! Follow orders! Focus, man! Focus!* Until finally: "At ease, sailor. As you were." Lunch!

TAKEAWAYS ───────────────────────────────

- **You are being followed**, even when you are following.
- **A learned follower** will become intimately involved with their own personal following process: the process by which you obtain, filter, store, and react to data.

- **The Pareto principle** (80/20 rule) posits that about 80 percent of data that comes to us is not as meaningful as the other 20 percent. There is a great deal of noise to filter.

- **Distractions come from all directions** in your psyche: logical, emotional, and instinctual (left, right, and root of the brain). Be alert.

- Our **biases are far reaching**, and they are ingrained in our brain at a chemical level from a very young age. They are far more than race, ethnicity, religion, gender, age, and so on.

- It is very difficult to **break the cycle of bias**. You must admit to it and then have to want to change it.

5

CURIOUS

"The more I learn, the more I realize I don't know."
—ALBERT EINSTEIN

I recall a time when I was trying to repair a sprinkler valve in the backyard. My dad, who was about seventy at the time, was at the house visiting and helping me in a way that only my dad could: using full-on brainpower. He was also moving as if we had all the time in the world, which was typical for him. I believe everyone in the family was preparing for some sort of celebration or gathering, and I just wanted to fix the damn thing and move on. But he would ask, "But how does it work?" "I don't know, Dad. And I don't care! This isn't a science project." My dad was not a scientist, for the record, but I bet he would have been good at it. In the name of expediency, I just changed some part in the sprinkler, and somehow it worked. I was done and ready to move on. But not my dad. "But wait! That doesn't make any sense. Why did that work? I want to know how it works!" For the rest of the day and evening, I could see the wheels turning in his head, working it all out. My dad, God rest his soul, the ever curious.

Fewer and fewer people, unlike my dad, seem to reach the fourth degree: the "curious" degree. As I mentioned earlier, the third degree—learned—is where most of us start to believe we know it all and stop applying our reason. This is the core idea of the theory: We are constantly following, whether we realize it or not.

We begin with instinct, then we're taught that following is good and necessary, and eventually reach the degree where we teach ourselves and others to do the same. At this point, we often put the process on autopilot, repeating what we've learned without thinking. It's like knowing multiplication tables: When we say 4 x 6 = 24, we're not consciously adding four six times or six four times; we simply know the answer. Following works the same way—automatically, without question.

However, those who reach the fourth degree—"curiosity"— break this cycle. These people are highly skilled. They employ reason and, as a result, teach others to use their reason too. Curiosity drives them. They understand their innate drive, that the world doesn't revolve around them, and constantly ask questions, especially of themselves. They are adept at identifying and eliminating distractions and eliminating bias. If they hold leadership positions, they excel because their approach to following is practiced, reasoned, and informed by a curious mindset.

There is a growing body of research in the field of curiosity. In a 2015 paper published in *Neuron*, authors Celeste Kidd and Benjamin Hayden provide a comprehensive history and analysis of curiosity.[1] While the subject is complex (as both the brain and psychology are), I want to offer a simpler, layperson's interpretation.

At its core, curiosity can be defined as "the impulse toward better cognition," a concept attributed to philosopher and psychologist William James.[2] For our discussion, it's important to focus on the term *cognition* rather than the word *desire*. This distinction matters because, while many would agree that all living beings exhibit some degree of curiosity, there's a difference between instinctive reactions and cognitive curiosity. For instance, when something catches a dog's attention, it investigates out of instinct. The well-known scientist Ivan Pavlov referred to this as a *reflex* rather than a *curiosity*.

On the other hand, humans may wonder about something— even ponder. But that is not what I mean by *curious*. Curiosity, as I mean it, is a desire to know and understand—cognition. The folks with this advanced followership skill set embrace the attribute with more intensity than most people. They know that whatever they discover will only lead to more questions for them to energetically pursue. It is a different level of curiosity that comes along with you at every stage of life. There is a difference between wanting the answer versus wanting to *understand* how the answer was derived—the answer *to* the answer. You can see the inherent loop here, yes? This reasoning is what led me to believe that curiosity is an advanced degree in people who "follow with reason."

At the "informed" stage of your followship development, limits are put upon your quest for resolution, muting your desire for understanding. The limits may be our own mental capabilities, as you are focused more on wonder than understanding, but the limits may also be components of necessity or societal norms. For example, a parent is never going to be able to successfully explain changing weather patterns to a child. The child has not developed the brainpower to grasp the concept yet. Added to that cognitive capacity is the stress of daily time as you try to get them dressed and out the door in the morning. The issue of time affects educators when they take the approach that some components must be simply memorized as fact without pursuit of the knowledge or reasoning that makes them facts in the first place.

Still, curiosity is ever present. But expedience, as with the sprinkler repair example, is inherent in the learned stage of development and, typically, we look to satiate our curiosity with the quickest, most expedient answer (another product of our miser brains). The goal of complete comprehension and understanding is set aside in the interest of time. Most often, it is left there. That is why I say that the curiosity degree of followship is rarely obtained—curiosity as a quest for reason.

One reason why it might be rarely obtained is because we still don't understand it well. What we know about the research on brain interaction and curiosity is still in its infancy. Scientists have not identified a reward system, neurochemically speaking, for curiosity. Perhaps it is a compulsion, or a talent people are born with, which they advance with exercise. Whatever the answer, I believe that to be an elite follower, curiosity and its two components are critical: a troubleshooting mindset and patience. Curiosity, in the way I'm using it, provides opportunities rather than answers or a destination. Elite followers want to understand how things work and are rarely satisfied. They crave not only knowledge but understanding, comprehension, and reasoning. They even post-evaluate their own conclusions (reflection). They don't just wonder, they solve. Therefore, the elite, even when faced with common, day-to-day time constraints, push back.

Here are a couple of examples of this curious mindset playing out today. In Douglas Ready's *MIT Sloan Management Review* article, the author notes that Alan Mulally and Larry Fink have very different management styles and personalities, though both men attribute equal importance to the role of curiosity.[3] Mulally was the former CEO of Ford and Boeing, and Fink the CEO of BlackRock. Both are phenomenally successful men. But read what is written about them in this article: "Fink describe[d] himself as a perpetual student who always asked questions" and "[Mulally] started by asking his team why people weren't buying Fords anymore. He wanted to understand the root cause." You see the pattern? The perpetual student, always asking questions and searching for *the answer to the answer*.

These are traits of an elite follower. Even the famous Elon Musk, whose curiosity is undeniable, is noted as saying, "In terms of a day-to-day habit, I think being curious about the world and how the world works—curious about everything really. I think curiosity is an extremely important thing to have. And [we need] to be somewhat obsessive about that curiosity. Probably obsessive curiosity is the number one [daily habit]."[4]

Think. Think. Think.

Winnie-the-Pooh, that little stuffed bear always on the hunt for honey, was one of my favorite cartoon characters when I was growing up. He was always working hard to think, as if reminding us kids: *think*. My dad had a similar phrase he used frequently: "Use your head!" Now that I'm an adult, I find myself telling my kids the same thing. I explain it like this: "If I told you to drop and give me fifty push-ups, that would be physically challenging, right? Your arms would strain, your stomach muscles would tighten, your back would hurt, your breathing and heart rate would increase, and you would sweat profusely. All of this because you were trying to make your body do something difficult. If your brain could sweat when you use it, then it would!"

Just as bodybuilders strain their muscles through exercise to make them bigger and stronger, athletes requiring speed, such as tennis players and sprinters, strengthen the neural pathways that control their muscle reactions. Repetitive exercise improves not just muscles but the brain's ability to process information quickly and efficiently. By exercising your brain, you're straining and strengthening the neural pathways, making them faster and stronger, thus making you smarter and helping you follow with reason more efficiently.[5]

Elite followers understand this principle and embrace it. That is why they are also successful leaders. These successful leaders are voracious readers. Reading is brain exercise. Note-taking is brain exercise. This kind of neurological growth (neuroplasticity) is not just limited to learning the subject matter. You are exercising your brain, making it stronger and faster for the next subject or topic, not just the current one. Simply by reading, you are building "superhighways" in your brain.

If you think of it that way, roads take us to many destinations—the more roads and the better quality of roads there are create more and better-quality pathways, yes? In the introduction, I listed famous leaders who are known for their love of reading. Most notable to me was Abraham Lincoln who, it is said, taught himself how to read.[6] That could not have been easy. Reading, whether self-taught or not, is a chore. I remember when I was young, if the family was going to play a new board game, we would all volunteer Dad to read the instructions because none of us wanted to put in the effort. "Besides, he likes to read," we told ourselves. But did he *actually* like to read, or did he *make* himself read? Anyway, we figured it was too hard to think about. My miser brain took the easiest and most expedient route to come to that conclusion. My brain instantaneously deduced that reading and comprehension were easy for my dad, that it just came to him naturally. I grew up admiring my father's brainpower.

Only now, in retrospect, do I recall that he was always reading something, anything—books, newspapers, even instructions to board games. He put effort into it. You must put effort into following with reason. You must *think* about it. I cannot overemphasize the idea that thinking hard about something, no matter what the topic, helps build, maintain, and reinforce your brainpower for use in more ways than the topic or effort you may be presently undertaking.

My mother used to love to do puzzles—another brain exercise. Have you noticed their prolific use as a therapeutic tool among the elderly now? I believe with the unfortunate increase in dementia and Alzheimer's in our elderly populations, more attention has been brought to the neurological benefit of working puzzles. It's good brainercise! Completing a picture puzzle requires the use of both the logical and creative sides of our brain. One must be organized and simultaneously detailed-oriented and big picture–oriented. And one must be persistent. Elite followers crave cognition stimuli, and that is just how a puzzle presents itself. It is about the challenge. Music presents the same challenge at an even higher level. In her research on neuroplasticity in a clinical setting, Joyce Shaffer notes several prominent studies where music, which simultaneously requires creativity and executive functions, has been shown to exercise several regions of the brain, including "cognitive skills of attention, control, motor function, visual scanning, and executive functioning."[7] Thus, both puzzles and music work both sides of the brain.

One of my favorite jobs also involved working both sides of

the brain. I was working as an aircraft electrician when I was in the navy. Our job rating had the initialism "AE," which me and my fellow aircraft electricians used to say stands for "aviation everything." This is because it seemed to us that whenever an aircraft came back with something wrong, we were always sent in first to determine which shop needed to fix the issue. Was it mechanical, hydraulic, electronics, electrical, or pilot error? We were troubleshooters extraordinaire. Problem-solvers. Each case was different, and each required a unique solution. But we followed a repeatable troubleshooting process, which at the core required a quest for reason—comprehending how things worked.

In the end, this is what an elite follower with reason lives for: comprehension, thinking, solving problems, approaching things from different perspectives. But what are you following then, you might ask? Since every case is different, each requires a unique solution. This is why we have to look at the process to answer the question about the relationship between trouble-shooting and following. With the puzzle, the first thing we do is frame the puzzle; frame the problem. We look at what was done before. In this case we look at the picture, then color, shape, patterns, and so on. When I was working on an aircraft, I would mimic the process of a scientist. I would first look at history and search for previous examples or patterns. What have others done before me when they were presented with a similar issue? I would attempt to isolate the issue and perform controlled experiments. I would follow this pattern of troubleshooting, which, at its core, is a quest for comprehension. Remember, *sequi cum ratione* is about the *process* of following—meaning with reason, not the resulting solution. The desire to understand the problem itself is what instigates the process of using our reason for these decisions.

In chapter 4, I talked about those in the "learned" degree, who do not use their reason. This degree forgets about the "reason" part, and many of us end up blindly moved along. I used the examples of solving a puzzle and troubleshooting an aircraft malfunction, but the matured follower can apply the same processes to whatever they are following, so long as it is a reasoned process. In solving the problem or issue, or deciding what or who to follow, if we want to apply reason to our discovery, we must always first strive to eliminate distractions and biases to get us to a legitimate level of curiosity. I may be following the work that was done before me, but at the same time, I am not blindly tied to it. That would be a form of bias. Thus, people at the "curiosity" stage with reason continually self-evaluate.

The bottom line about curiosity is that it is good to ask questions—not for the sake of the answer, but for comprehension—understanding. Curiosity as a degree of followship should never be confused with wonder. If you are truly curious, you will strive for understanding and work until you obtain it. This takes work. It requires us to think, think, think.

Patience

I often think about singer–songwriter Tom Petty's "The Waiting." Waiting is difficult, isn't it? There is a reason that patience is a virtue. If you've made it to this point in the book, you have exercised some patience yourself. Thank you. I pray that it has been time well spent. Now, as with the other degrees of *sequi cum ratione*, this one is challenging and requires work. Especially in a day and age where speed is held in such high demand, patience is exceedingly difficult to come by. We have been conditioned to be *impatient*. Delayed gratification? Forget about it. But it's so necessary to exercise patience in following with reason. Along with thinking things through when solving problems, patience makes up the second lever in the curiosity of the elite follower.

Patience is a powerful virtue. I think of my history in the accounting and finance field, when all the auditors and government examiners would ask me questions in the course of their work, and then they would wait so patiently, in silence, even after I had answered. They were waiting to see if I had anything else to add. Think of the lawyers in the movies you've seen, or great detective characters: They patiently wait to see if their opponent will squirm under the stillness of patience and break, divulging some crucial piece of information. Patience is power. The word is mentioned about seventy times in the Bible and is considered a fruit of the Holy Spirit. To be curious at this level, you have to be a very patient thinker. How many times have you heard someone say to someone else, "You are so patient!" as if it is a superhuman power?

As with curiosity, there is limited research and experimentation into the neuroscience behind patience. Katsuhiko Miyazaki, at the Okinawa Institute of Science and Technology Graduate University, published a study in the journal *Nature Communications* that pointed to the role that serotonin plays in increasing patience in mice.[8] It appears that the dorsal raphe nucleus of the frontal cortex of the brain, the primary generator of serotonin, somehow grasps the idea of delayed gratification and can increase or decrease its output based on an expected reward. But, as I said, more work needs to be done.

Nevertheless, as with curiosity and following with reason, I am really speaking to a deeper level of the character trait known as *patience*. When I think of professions that require a great deal of patience—such as scientist, surgeon, teacher— those who appear to be successful are individuals who exhibit extraordinary patience. Most likely they even exhibited this special quality in their childhood, like they would any other talent. But as with any talent, if it goes unexercised, it's a waste. Do you remember that a skill is learned and improved through exercise and practice? The same rule applies to talents.

Looking back at what we have covered here in the book, it seems clear to me that the simple act of reasoning, in and of itself, involves a great deal of patience—left brain, right brain, back of the brain, our logical side, emotional side, and instinctual self. Sure, we are smart creatures, but there are so many inputs to filter through, and the amount seems to increase at an astronomical rate. Our brains need time to process. Do we put those filters to work with thorough reasoning to follow well? I don't think we do. I believe that is why so many of us are willing to blindly follow others. And I believe, to a great extent, the reason so many of us follow rashly, as opposed to *rationally*, is because of a lack of patience. Even the cooking shows on TV are about speed. Julia Child is probably turning in her grave at the emphasis placed on speed cooking. Nowadays, it seems, the word *patience* has a bad rap, like *following*. *Patience* is often misinterpreted as *lazy, lethargic, slow, inactive,* or *indecisive*. What about *methodical, steady, thorough, calculating, calm, logical,* and so on? Good things take time. And nothing worth having is easy.

Recently, I tried my hand at propagating a fiddle-leaf fig tree. Propagation is a process wherein you cut off a branch, remove the bottom leaves, skim off some bark at the end of the branch, and then try to get it to start growing roots of its own. I cut two branches and, as an experiment, put one branch in a clear vase filled with water and the other in a container of soil. Full disclosure, I also used some root stimulator. It took well over a month before I started seeing roots on the branch in the vase. I had thought it was a complete failure. All that time, the plant gave me no feedback—it didn't move, it didn't even say thank you! At the same time, I was so curious as to what was going on with the other branch, in the container. I wanted to pull it up and see if there were roots on the branch or not. *Patience, Bob, patience.* Sure enough, it was two months or more before I started seeing new growth on the top of the branch in the container. It seemed to take forever!

Another personal example is the process I underwent in creating this book. I recently told an old friend about me working on it. He reminded me that I had actually been talking about this theory back in high school. At that time, I had dubbed it "The False Truth." I suppose that means it has been fifty years in the "patient" making. When you achieve success or breakthroughs, or simply complete a project, to others it may appear to be an overnight success. I have read that it took Darwin decades to solidify his idea of evolution. *Decades.* Talk about patience. Looking in from the outside, people do not know that what appears to be sudden has been years or even decades in the making. This is true in every discipline, from the arts to engineering, science to theology, and even philosophy.

We have done so much to get to this point, striving to define a path to *sequi cum ratione*. We've put in the work. We focused on the big picture and took the long view while keeping an eye on the details. We have defined the degrees and levers within them. And now, the last ingredient is patience.

TAKEAWAYS

- Curiosity is, at a fundamental level, "the impulse toward better cognition"; not to be confused with *wonder*. This is **a desire to not just know, but to understand**. A quest for comprehension.

- These two components of curiosity are critical: **a troubleshooting mindset and patience.**

- **Thinking is exercise for your brain (brainercise).** It strains the neural pathways and synapses, making them faster and stronger, thus making you smarter and a faster follower with reason. Reading, taking notes, doing puzzles, playing musical instruments, and fixing things are all brain exercise.

- The drive to **want to understand the problem itself** is what instigates the process of following with reason.

- We have been conditioned to be *impatient*. But **it is necessary to exercise patience in following with reason.**

- **Focus on the big picture** and take the long view while working to understand the details. Think of the entire picture of the puzzle while trying to decipher that one piece of the puzzle.

- An elite follower is patient, though patience is often mistaken for being lazy, lethargic, slow, inactive, or indecisive. **For the elite follower, patience means being methodical, steady, thorough, calculating, calm, logical, and so on.**

6

VULNERABILITY

If at any time during your reading of this book you've thought, *I need to give this to someone because they're following the wrong path*, take a moment to examine that impulse. Believing that someone else is wrong—and that you're in a position to correct them—implies you think you are on the *right* path. If that sounds familiar, the central idea of this final degree of followship—"vulnerability"—might be challenging for you to accept. It's like "the longest yard," as they say. Have you questioned yourself? You must always consider the possibility that you've made a mistake along the way. When I am cooking and following a recipe, I find myself constantly doubling back and making sure I read that right—was it a teaspoon or a tablespoon?

Baking soda or powder? When following, we must consistently question our own reasoning.

I could be wrong, of course (practicing vulnerability), but I believe that throughout history, reasoned vulnerability is the one trait consistently demonstrated by the greatest followers. Remember the steps that got us to this point: acknowledging our instinct in this area, active listening and asking questions, removing distractions and biases, exercising our brains, and having patience. The final step is practicing reasoned vulnerability—the pinnacle degree of *sequi cum ratione*. Not *vulnerable* the adjective, but *vulnerability* the noun. More directly, the *exercising* of the noun—to *practice* vulnerability.

Remember the opening story where, at age fifteen, I willingly walked into an abusive situation? Most people would say that a person at that age is still weak in all human aspects—physically, emotionally, spiritually—and this makes them a *vulnerable* person. In general, a lack of power in one sense or another is what is commonly regarded as *being vulnerable*. And in the sense that I was powerless in that situation, it is true that I was vulnerable: I was an easy target. I *was* vulnerable in the sense of being at the mercy of someone more powerful, but I was not *practicing* vulnerability—certainly not *reasoned* vulnerability. I was already vulnerable when the trap was set. The predator knew I would follow the other boy (instinct degree). And he knew I would follow the instructions of authority (informed degree). The leap to practicing reasoned vulnerability was far beyond my youth (which is why I advocate for teaching the concept beginning in middle school).

The concept of "practicing vulnerability," for our purposes, means *intentionally* putting yourself in a position of vulnerability by way of *reasoning*. We can call it "reasoned vulnerability." This is not only shedding your ego but being open to the possibility that your vulnerability may lead to some personal harm—physically, mentally, or emotionally—*when it is required, in the service of reason*. And it means accepting the consequences. Don't be confused here. I am certainly not stating that I was practicing reasoned vulnerability in my youth. In fact, it was the opposite. There was no reasoning involved whatsoever. Rather, to grasp this concept, think of two elite followers of our time: Mohandas Gandhi and Martin Luther King Jr. Both men employed reasoned vulnerability by following at an elite level to achieve their desired outcomes of securing India's independence from Great Britian and of civil rights for Black Americans, respectively. Their employing nonviolence to achieve their means meant they were vulnerable to great physical, mental, and emotional harm, eventually leading to their assassinations. They practiced reasoned vulnerability, walking in the steps of the religious and secular heroes that had come before them.[1]

Practicing Vulnerability

Vulnerability in followship is inherently elusive. Unlike the other degrees of followship, it is not a stage we can all master. Instead, it is an inherently transient stage, one that even the most curious and elite may struggle to practice consistently in all areas of their lives. If you manage to achieve vulnerability in one instance, you can easily lose it in the next. Vulnerability, in this context, is a very difficult trait to master consistently. It requires striking a balance that changes during every experience in your life. Even if you find yourself able to consistently practice vulnerability in one arena of your life—at work, in relationships, in parenting— you may one day find yourself presented with a situation that tests your ability to practice vulnerability.

Here is a work-life example of the difficulty of practicing vulnerability. A person I know—I'll call him "the boss"—accepted a new job. One of the first tasks put before the boss by his own hierarchy was to fire one of the employees under his authority. The employee was set to be fired for an error he was partially responsible for. However, the boss was accustomed to acting honorably and rationally during his career, so he did his due diligence and researched the error before terminating the employee. Once he did some digging, he found the circumstances of the employee's so-called error were rather inconclusive. In fact, the boss determined, there was enough ambiguity with respect to the process, others involved, and the chain of authority that he reasoned it was unfair to fire the employee. The boss shared his conclusions with upper management, but they insisted some action must be taken. "*Someone* needs to pay for the mistake" was the entirety of their thought process.

The boss felt conflicted. He considered putting his own job on the line. He could refuse to terminate the employee and tell upper management, "If he goes, I go," essentially sacrificing his new job for the sake of what he reasoned was an injustice. But ultimately, the boss could not make that leap. He could not make himself that vulnerable. That is what I mean by *practicing vulnerability*. Now, you may ask, in that scenario, what or who was the boss following? Clearly, he followed his orders and fired his employee. Recall in the chapter on "learned" followship I stated that many people who find themselves in a leadership role plateau in the learned degree, resting in that role and forgetting they are followers for life. People may still advance within the leadership hierarchy, but they are not effective leaders in the long run if they don't move to the next degrees: "curious" and "vulnerability."

The boss chose the "leaders" above him, all of whom were, sadly, not using their reason. At that learned degree, they are stuck in the power, authority, and self-preservation mode, unable to eliminate distractions and break free of the bias infinity loop.

Granted, it is difficult to do. They could not move on to the next degree, "curious," where thinking things through and embracing patience are key tenets. The boss and his superiors reasoned their way to a false truth, thinking that somehow firing this individual at the bottom of the chain of command would protect them under the guise of "justice." In the long run, it did not hold true.

Here's a less serious example, but one I believe applies easily to our discussion. Paul McCartney of The Beatles has said about playing the bass, "The bass player was normally a fat guy who stood at the back. In our minds it was the fat guy in the group nearly always played the bass, and he stood at the back. None of us wanted that. We wanted to be up front, singing, looking good. That was what we wanted, to pull the birds [girls]."[2] Paul is a known songwriter, multi-instrumentalist, and vocalist. Some would say a musical genius. I think he had to practice some reasoned vulnerability there in that decision to take up the bass for the sake of the band and the music. He didn't even own his own bass at the time. But he later embraced it, calling out James Jamerson and Brian Wilson as his "two biggest influences."[3]

Vulnerability Versus Humility

Humility and *vulnerability* are similar concepts, but not the same. Let's start with humility. In high school, a teacher and mentor taught me about types of humility. As we were discussing the subject of falsities in life, he explained to me the concept of "false humility." This teacher was a good man, by my estimation. To illustrate his point, he said, "If a pretty girl is with her friends preening in front of the mirror and says, 'Oh, I am so ugly,' or, 'I am so fat,' when clearly she is neither—that is not humility. It can be many other things, but it is not humility. It could be insecurity or even pride, calling negative attention to herself in the hopes of receiving compliments from her well-intentioned friends." In this example, the pretty girl's statement isn't a reflection of her real, authentic feelings but a means to some other end—receiving validation, attention, and so on. This false humility is not what we are after. But you see it play out in the workplace as well, under the guise of servant leadership—a philosophy that is centuries old. Adages such as, "Don't boast about yourself or take all the credit," "Admit your mistakes," "I'm the stupidest person in the room," and, "The buck stops here" already abound in leadership circles, although they offer little in the way of true humility and are far from the true practice of reasoned vulnerability. It's almost as if people who espouse such advice believe that simply checking the humility box will get people to follow you out of sympathy. It is used as just another strategy to manipulate peoples' emotions and amass power and control rather than an earnest desire to follow and be followed with reason. Instead, our reason must guide our emotions. Those who use this false humility to manipulate are being insincere; they miss the point entirely. Elite level followers are not after power; they are after wisdom.

Genuine humility has been touted recently in many popular books and talks on leadership. For example, in *Daring Greatly*, Dr. Brené Brown writes of the need for leaders to be courageous and vulnerable, saying, "Being vulnerable and open is mutual and an integral part of the trust-building process."[4] I agree. But I believe it stops short of addressing the difference between being truly humble and this concept of practicing vulnerability. Getting closer to the concept is found in *Good to Great*, where author Jim Collins describes level 5 (top level) executive leadership as a "paradoxical blend of personal humility and professional will."[5] This concept dovetails with practicing vulnerability because he calls out "professional will." Let me expound. For our purposes here, and for ease of explanation, I would describe *humility* as based in emotion, while *vulnerability* is based in action. Having said that, I don't believe you can practice vulnerability without being humble. You *can* be humble and not take it to the next level of practicing vulnerability. I believe it takes humility to admit a mistake and say you're sorry. But to truly learn from the experience and, more importantly, make a change and embrace that change, then we are entering the realm of practicing vulnerability.

In the 1982 film *Gandhi*, there is a scene that takes place during the partition of India, when Muslims and Hindus were fighting each other. A Hindu man comes to Gandhi seeking forgiveness for killing a Muslim boy. The man is humble in that he recognizes he did wrong, and he is remorseful, asking for forgiveness. But Gandhi requires more from him. Gandhi wants the man to be vulnerable (perhaps as the boy he killed was vulnerable), and he instructs the Hindu man to find an orphaned Muslim boy and raise him as his own. But further, he tells him to raise that boy in the Muslim faith—not the man's faith, Hindu, but the Muslim faith. To do so would cause the man to find great strength within himself, challenging him not only physically but mentally and even spiritually.[6] We don't know, in the movie, if he was able to handle the challenge, to practice that level of vulnerability, but it is a great illustration. It reminds me of the parable of the rich man who wanted to follow Jesus. He was committed until Jesus told him to sell everything he owned and give it to the poor, then follow Him. "At that statement his face fell, and he went away sad, for he had many possessions."[7] Practicing vulnerability is tough.

When it comes to the role of humility when practicing reasoned vulnerability, two variables are at play: your sincerity and the ability of others to be reasoned followers. You can take care of your own sincerity, but as we have discussed, many people—including most people in leadership roles—are not reasoned. Hence the admiration of dictators in the present day and age. Do you think dictators are elite? They are not. Nor are their followers. In the long run, the dictator's time in a leadership role will be doomed, sometimes catastrophically so. They are forever stuck in the "learned" degree of followship, unable to remove distractions and get out of the bias infinity loop, unable to think things through, unable to practice patience and vulnerability. These things are far, far beyond their grasp—if they even desire to grasp them. Yet, people still choose these kinds of leaders willingly. Why? Because it takes *effort* to follow with reason! It is simply the miser brain at work: It is easier and most expedient to avoid engaging our reason.

The only reasoned approach you can have, then, to this inevitability of human nature is to embrace the fact that who is following you is not as important as who and what you are following. Focus on yourself. This is where the reasoned practice of vulnerability comes into play. I believe it takes a good amount of actual and sincere reasoning to see the reality of the fact that it took an infinite number of variables to get you into the seat you are in—most of which were not of your own making. There are people who, without sincerity, go through false attempts at appearing humble, who don't take the seat at the head of the table or don't speak until last, or who may say, "I'm the stupidest person in the room," and so on. They do and say these things with an undertone of insincerity. As another example, undoubtedly you have heard, "Let me play devil's advocate for a minute." Be assured, the moment someone says those words, they are *not* acting in that capacity. The real goal of the people in all these examples is to call attention to themselves and their performative show of humility where their true focus is on who is following them.

Someone who, regardless of their performative actions, really thinks deep down that they deserve to be at the head of the table, or to speak and be heard, is not humble. To be capable of true humility, you must believe, in your heart and mind, that in any given situation you are thankful to be at the table at all. You are not concerned with who is following you. To put your own mind, heart, and soul in this obvious state of weakness is practicing vulnerability. It can be risky. You must use reason, not emotion, to attain this level of belief—to understand that you have much to learn by listening to others. I have been told by acting and vocal coaches that the audience can tell what you are thinking. They know what you are saying to yourself in your mind and heart; it comes through. False humility screams its presence. Rather, to take humility to the next level, the level of reasoned vulnerability, let "I must decrease" be your mantra—and mean it.

Power and the quest for power run counter to following with

reason. You have likely heard the expression, "Love is a verb." The same is true of vulnerability—it's something you actively practice. To illustrate, consider the example of forgiveness. When someone says, "I can forgive, but I will not forget," they are still clinging to power. It may be a negative form of power, but it's power nonetheless—the power of memory, which can be used as leverage or as a weapon. That is not true forgiveness.

The difference between this and complete forgiveness lies in the practice of vulnerability, where power is willingly surrendered. True forgiveness is the complete release of power, memory, and emotions like resentment, bitterness, anger, hurt, and even—perhaps especially—judgment. In their place, you cultivate compassion, benevolence, love, and mercy. I have applied this practice in my own life, and it takes a great deal of vulnerability to admit you've been on the wrong path. It also requires a significant mental effort to reach this level of vulnerability. If you are concerned about being defined as a leader, remember, in the long run, those who practice reasoned vulnerability come out on top.

Following with Vulnerability

How, then, should you practice vulnerability in your progress toward following with reason? While this book is not rooted in religion, there are aspects of religiosity within the concept, and these are most evident when vulnerability is fully embraced. Religions, in essence, involve following someone or something, and their devotees are often willing to sacrifice themselves in that pursuit.

Take, for instance, John the Baptist—a prime example of this kind of vulnerability. Though "just a man" in Christian theology, he was considered the greatest man born of a woman and was a successful leader, with many disciples and even more who came to see him minister.[8] His power was so significant that it ultimately cost him his life. Still, at the peak of his influence, John the Baptist said, "I must decrease."[9] In that moment, he practiced the ultimate form of vulnerability, showing us reason at its highest level.

This pinnacle of vulnerability does not only apply to religion and spirituality, but everyday life as well. There was a time when I worked in an environment where drinking in excess was normal, an expected part of playing the game. And "playing the game" is just another way of saying "following the leader without reason." There was "the game" as I *wanted* to see it, which played nicely into the addiction that I was born with. This combination of my baseline and my alcohol-soaked work environment served to generate a false reasoning—a false truth. I reasoned that everyone was doing it. In reality, everyone was *not* doing it, and drinking was *not* a requirement for success. I lived the expression, "My reality is my truth." I reasoned myself into pursuing the wrong thing, and that was the easy part. This is an example of why you always need to reflect on your reasoning for doing something, because realities change. A priest once told me, "Be careful . . . self-perception can easily be confused with self-deception." Sage advice passed on from his mom. At any rate, eventually, I questioned my reasoning in the case of drinking to fit in, which allowed me—in a state of reasoned vulnerability—to admit I needed to get out of the loop I had created with my flawed reasoning. I realized that I must sacrifice my ego, surrender to the reasoned truth, and seek another path. That act of admitting my error was an act of vulnerability.

Looking back to when I was fifteen and walking into an abusive situation, I was already vulnerable through instinct and learned degrees of following without reason. Being vulnerable *without* reason was easy, even natural. That's why children are often easy prey: They haven't learned the hard part yet. The hard part is practicing *reasoned* vulnerability. Had I been taught how to reason this way in my youth, it probably would not have prevented me from obeying authority at that age, but it might have led me to share what happened with my parents instead of keeping it to myself. I had the power to make that decision, but I thought speaking up would only lead to humiliation, which

I was not willing to risk. I hadn't been taught how to practice reasoned vulnerability, so I reasoned myself into a false truth.

In hindsight, it seems obvious how reasoned vulnerability plays out in many arenas of life, often in the simplest of ways: confessing a mistake or betrayal in a relationship, knowing and admitting your weaknesses to others, coming clean about a choice you came to regret in parenting, trying to take back a word or a phrase you've mistakenly uttered in front of your children, or letting your kids see you ask others for help. I remember a time in my life when I would not admit that I was lost. Rather, I would say, "I am not lost. I am just dis-located!" It became a joke, but I believe that I taught my children—always watching—a way to deceive, a way of telling a false truth, and a path of pride. Your children will follow your example (especially during their "informed" degree). In life, we must admit—*and believe*—that we don't know everything, that what was taught to us in our lifetime could be wrong or that we could be wrong, that someone else most likely knows more, and that we have made and continue to make mistakes. And then, most importantly, we must be willing to act—adjust, revisit, make amends, fail, fail *again*, fall, and get back up. We must be willing to practice reasoned vulnerability and ask for help. These things feel painful in our hearts and minds, but there is no better way of following with reason.

TAKEAWAYS ────────────────────────────────

- **Practicing reasoned vulnerability** means intentionally putting yourself in the position of being vulnerable by way of "reasoning." Think of elite followers of our time: Mohandas Gandhi and Martin Luther King Jr.

- **Vulnerability in followship is inherently elusive.** Even if you manage to achieve it in one instance, it is easily lost in the next.

- **Reason over emotion.**

- Watch out anytime you feel like **"my reality is my truth."** This mindset can lead to a false truth and unreasoned following. **Realities change.**

- **Revisit conclusions**—you must constantly revisit what you consider to be your reasoned following decisions.

- The hard part of practicing vulnerability in following with reason is *admitting* **when you are following the** *wrong thing* **and then** *taking action.*

- Let **"I must decrease"** be your mantra—and mean it.

CONCLUSION

FOLLOWSHIP FOR LIFE

Why is *sequi cum ratione* important? It is simple, really. You are a born follower, and you will die a follower, so it's better—and more fully human—to follow with reason. It sounds simple, but we usually think we *are* already using our reason in this way. Yet, many of us do not. We are unaware of this dependency because all our lives we have been taught—*conditioned*—to follow *without* reason. Our miser brains, being the efficient neuroplastic organs they are, really like it that way. It's easier to default to going along with whoever and whatever is around us, however we were raised, whoever and whatever demands our attention the most insistently—but the consequences of such a path that fails to use reason are often greater than simple unoriginality. You don't want to find yourself falling off a cliff because you were following blindly.

Using that head of yours to its fullest capability requires you to conceptualize followship as a lifelong skill set that can be developed, taught, and practiced, much like leadership. But this skill is a much more pervasive concept than leadership: No one is a born leader, but *everyone* is a born follower. If you fail to develop your skill set and do not advance beyond the very basic instinctual, informed, and learned degrees that our society trains in us, you will become accustomed to doing so without reason. In a very tangible way, we are all taught to obey blindly . . . to follow without reason. The solution to this default path resides in the five degrees of followship development, which can be utilized to sharpen your ability progress with reason: "instinctual," "informed," "learned," "curious," and "vulnerability."

Using reason in this way does not run counter to leadership; rather, it takes its place as both predecessor and complement to leadership. The greatest leaders are the greatest followers with reason. I challenge anyone to point to an individual in any field who consistently achieved great and enduring success but did not demonstrate the characteristics of an elite follower throughout their lives, such as avid reading or genuine curiosity. Following with reason does not limit your ingenuity, creativeness, wisdom, or strength. Instead, it serves as a lever to boost your capability in all these facets of your cognition. As with any other skill, it is one that should be acknowledged, disciplined, and exercised with rigor.

Knowing this, you can make the conscious effort to rewire your brain and engage your reason, or you can stay the course and be blown this way or that by the winds of fads, false truth, or the strong personalities you encounter throughout life. But all those people will also be following something or someone else who is *sequi sin ratione*—following without reason. Decide what or who you will follow by first deciding *the process* by which you will do so and employ a *reasoned* strategy.

In the end, it's all about exercising our brains. You must *want* to do it and *choose* to work at it; otherwise, your miser brain will default to taking the easy route. The damage caused by following without reason has generational effects, not simply in trauma but in biases and conditioned loyalties where there should be none—from family feuds to politics to wars. Circumstances change and our thought processes need to change with them—with reason, effort, and sacrifice. While most readers will do this in their adult life, we must work to break the cycle of unreasoned following by teaching our children the stoic reasoning path as well. Knowing that they will mimic you, model for them how to use their reason. *Sequi cum ratione.* Go now and make a positive difference in the world, one life and one mind at a time—starting with your own. Good luck. Godspeed.

ACKNOWLEDGMENTS

I have a daily prayer where I humbly ask God to cleanse my mind, purify my heart, and heal my body; that God may abide in me, and I in God, and that I make a positive difference in at least one person's life that day. I have been praying that prayer since I don't know when. Interestingly, it is only in the writing of this book that I have come to realize that I don't thank God enough for the ones who have come before me. Specifically, the ones I have followed . . . the people who have directly made a difference in my life. My parents, to whom this book is dedicated, are at the top of the list. I am saddened that they have recently passed and will not see the published book. But I do vividly remember telling my dad about it before the Alzheimer's set in. I will cherish the memory of his engaging eyes and questioning mind. Of course, I also cherish the memory of my mom, whose indefatigable and unconditional love, confidence, and ceaseless prayers sustained me on my journey of learning to follow with reason. I didn't mention her in the book (she would have wanted it that way), but her fingerprints are all over it.

I will also be eternally grateful for my loving and supportive spouse, partner, and best friend, Kari Camille (KC), who continues to use all her wisdom and strength to try and convince me that I still have something to offer this world. She is my greatest fan, and I owe her my life, literally (a story for another time).

And speaking of wisdom . . . other teachers of wisdom and following with reason to whom I owe my thanks and acknowledgment: Brother Richard Martins, S.M. (deceased)—the world doesn't revolve around me. Brother Joseph Francis (now Father Steven)—the virtue of being still. John Schuster—the importance of separating emotion from reason. Rob Harris—revealing the Seat of Wisdom and showing me that even the toughest and bravest of men should reach for her. Roland Ruiz, who reminded me of my "false-truth" thesis from high school, but also, more importantly, the importance of playing bass!

I would like to also acknowledge and thank all the folks at Greenleaf Book Group for their partnership and expert advice, particularly Amanda Elysse Hughes, whose professionalism and expertise in her craft as a writer and editor were instrumental to me, though I am especially thankful for her encouragement.

And, finally, I have an obvious thank-you to you, the reader. My hope and prayer is that the book makes at least a small difference in your life for the good. Honestly, though, either way, pass it on, because more likely than not, someone is following you. Smile. Be happy. Follow with reason! And God bless.

PS. For those of you who may also order the audiobook, please allow me to acknowledge Landis Chisenhall, owner/operator and chief engineer of Cibilo Studios in San Antonio, Texas, for his support, expertise, and especially his encouragement and patience during the audiobook production.

NOTES

Introduction

1. Xin Le Ng, Choi Sang Long, and Khairiah BINTI Soehod, "The Effects of Servant Leadership on Employee's Job Withdrawal Intention," *Asian Social Science* 12, no. 2 (January 2016): 2.

2. Mark 10:42–45 (English Standard Version).

3. The Business Research Company, *Corporate Training Global Market Report 2024*, January 2024, https://www.thebusinessresearchcompany.com/report/corporate-training-global-market-report#:~:text=The%20corporate%20training%20market%20size,(CAGR)%20of%204.6%25.

4. "Corporate Leadership Training Market to Hit USD 63.19 Billion by 2030 | Exclusive Report by Fortune Business Insights™," GlobeNewswire, December 13, 2023, https://www.globenewswire.com/news-release/2023/12/13/2795296/0/en/Corporate-Leadership-Training-Market-to-Hit-USD-63-19-Billion-by-2030-Exclusive-Report-by-Fortune-Business-Insights.html.

5. Kobra Movalled, Anis Sani, Leila Nikniaz, and Morteza Ghojazadeh, "The Impact of Sound Stimulations During Pregnancy on Fetal Learning: A Systematic Review," *BMC Pediatrics* 23, article no. 183 (April 2023), https://bmcpediatr.biomedcentral.com/articles/10.1186/s12887-023-03990-7.

6. Kierstan Boyd, "Vision Development: Newborn to 12 Months," American Academy of Ophthalmology, July 12, 2024, https:// www.aao.org/eye-health/tips-prevention/baby-vision-development-first-year.

7. Eric Martone, ed., *Royalists, Radicals, and les Misérables: France in 1832* (Newcastle upon Tyne, UK: Cambridge Scholars Publishing, 2013).

8. Konrad Lorenz, *Studies in Animal and Human Behavior,* vols. 1 and 2 (Harvard University Press, 1973, 1974). See also, Konrad Lorenz, *The Companion in the Environment of the Bird* (Harvard University Press, 1970).

9. Erwin Lemche, "Research Evidence from Studies on Filial Imprinting, Attachment, and Early Life Stress: A New Route for Scientific Integration," *Acta Ethologica* 23 (June 2020): 127–33.

10. Angela Hicks and Carolyn Korbel, "Attachment Theory," in *Encyclopedia of Behavioral Medicine*, eds. Marc Gellman and Rick Turner (Springer, 2013). See also, Julia Heyl, "Imprinting in Psychology," Verywellmind, June 9, 2023, https://www. verywellmind.com/imprinting-in-psychology-7504676.

11. Irving Janis, *Victims of Groupthink: A Psychological Study of Foreign-Policy Decisions and Fiascoes,* (Houghton Mifflin, 1972).

12. Oliver Pol, Todd Bridgman, and Stephen Cummings, "The Forgotten 'Immortalizer': Recovering William H. Whyte as the Founder and Future of Groupthink Research," *Human Relations* 75, no. 8 (August 2022): 1615–41, https://doi.org/10.1177/ 00187267211070680.

13. Pol, Bridgman, and Cummings, "The Forgotten 'Immortalizer.'"

14. Amy Shira Teitel, "What Caused the *Challenger* Disaster?" History.com, January 25, 2018, www.history.com/news/how-the-challenger-disaster-changed-nasa.

15. Solomon Asch, "Effects of Group Pressure upon the Modification and Distortion of Judgments," in *Groups, Leadership, and Men: Research in Human Relations*, ed. Harold Guetzkow (New York: Carnegie Press, 1951), 177–90.

16. Christian Jarrett, "Asch's 'Conformity Study' without the Confederates," The British Psychological Society, October 22, 2010, https://www.bps.org.uk/research-digest/aschs-conformity-study-without-confederates.

17. Stanley Milgram, "Behavioral Study of Obedience," *Journal of Abnormal and Social Psychology* 67, no. 4 (1963): 371–8.

18. Thomas Blass, "The Milgram Paradigm After 35 Years: Some Things We Now Know About Obedience to Authority," *Journal of Applied Social Psychology* 29, no. 5 (1999): 955–78.

19. Lexi Lonas Cochran, "McConnell Overestimated Number of GOP Senators Who'd Vote to Convict Trump: Book," The Hill, April 28, 2022, https://thehill.com/homenews/senate/3470612-mcconnell-overestimated-number-of-gop-senators-whod-vote-to-convict-trump-book/.

Chapter 1

1. John Greathouse, "Business Wisdom from the Master CEO: Lee Iacocca," Forbes.com, July 6, 2019, https://www.forbes.com/sites/johngreathouse/2019/07/06/business-wisdom-from-the-master-ceo-lee-iacocca/.

2. Abraham Maslow, "A Theory of Human Motivation," *Psychological Review* 50 (1943): 370–96.

3. "Nobel Prize Facts," The Nobel Prize, October 5, 2009, https://www.nobelprize.org/prizes/facts/nobel-prize-facts/.

4. Harvard University Press, "Lincoln's Reading Habits," Medium.com, February 12, 2019, https://hup.medium.com/lincolns-reading-habits-dc0b7adeede7.

5. "Jefferson and Books," The Jefferson Monticello, https://www. monticello.org/thomas-jefferson/a-day-in-the-life-of-jefferson/ sanctum-sanctorum/jefferson-and-books. See also, "Theodore Roosevelt's Libraries," Theodore Roosevelt Center, https://www. theodorerooseveltcenter.org/Learn-About-TR/TR-Encyclopedia/ Reading%20and%20Writing/Roosevelt%20Libraries.

6. Jonathan Rose, "Winston Churchill's Beach Reading: His Top Ten Books," Yale University Press, June 29, 2015, https://yalebooks. yale.edu/2015/06/29/winston-churchills-beach-reading-his-top-ten-books. See also, Ted Bromund, "Margaret Thatcher's Lesson: To Triumph, Do Your Homework," The Heritage Foundation, April 16, 2013, https://www.heritage.org/conservatism/commentary/ margaret-thatchers-lesson-triumph-do-your-homework. See also, Mihaela Culea, "Humanizing the Queen: Reading as Self-Discovery and Writing as Redemption in Alan Bennett's *The Uncommon Reader*," *Rupkatha Journal on Interdisciplinary Studies in Humanities* V, no. 3 (2013), https://rupkatha.com/ alan-bennetts-the-uncommon-reader. See also, Square Panda India, "Remembering Mahtama Gandhi, and His Thoughts on Education," Medium.com, October 2, 2020, https://medium. com/@squarepandaindia/remembering-mahatma-gandhi-and-his-thoughts-on-education-ac47cb8dcd79.

7. Nomadic Samuel, "How Warren Buffet's Reading Habits Contribute to His Success," Picture Perfect Portfolios, September 1, 2024, https://pictureperfectportfolios.com/how-warren-buffetts-reading-habits-contribute-to-his-success; Chris Weller, "9 of the Most Successful People Share Their Reading Habits," Business Insider, July 20, 2017, https://www.businessinsider.com/what-successful-people-read-2017-7. See also, "Billionaires and Their Reading Habits," The Wisdom Post, https://www.thewisdompost. com/reading/billionaires-and-their-reading-habits/1073.

8. Jeffrey Rosen, *The Pursuit of Happiness* (Simon & Schuster, 2024), 6.

9. Philippians 2 (ESV).

10. Philippians 2 (ESV).

11. "Army Leadership and the Profession," Army Doctrine Publication ("ADP") 6–22, Department of the Army, July 2019, https://armypubs.army.mil/epubs/DR_pubs/DR_a/ARN18529-ADP_6-22-000-WEB-1.pdf.

12. "Army Leadership and the Profession."

13. Philippians 2:3 (ESV).

Chapter 2

1. Susan Fiske and Shelley Taylor, *Social Cognition: From Brains to Culture* (McGraw-Hill, 1984). See also, Fritz Heider, *The Psychology of Interpersonal Relations* (John Wiley & Sons, 1958).

2. Dietrich Bonhoeffer, *Letters and Papers from Prison* (Touchstone, 1997).

3. *Hello, Dolly!*, directed by Gene Kelly (1968, Twentieth Century Studios).

4. "Anti-Japanese Propaganda," Naval History and Heritage Command, https://www.history.navy.mil/content/dam/museums/hrnm/Education/EducationWebsiteRebuild/AntiJapanesePropaganda/AntiJapanesePropagandaInfoSheet/Anti-Japanese%20Propaganda%20info.pdf.

Chapter 3

1. Mariam Arain, Maliha Haque, Lina Johal, Puja Mathur, Wynand Nel, Afsha Rais, Ranbir Sandhu, Sushil Sharma, "Maturation of the Adolescent Brain," *Neuropsychiatric Disease and Treatment* 9 (2013): 449–61.

2. Benedict Mayaki, "Education and Desire for Peace Highlighted at Pre-G20 Meetings," Vatican News, November 14, 2022, https://

www.vaticannews.va/en/world/news/2022-11/education-g20-b20-bali-indonesia-business-society.html.

3. Grace Lindsay, "Attention in Psychology, Neuroscience, and Machine Learning," *Frontiers in Computational Neuroscience* 14 (April 2020), https://www.frontiersin.org/journals/computational-neuroscience/articles/10.3389/fncom.2020.00029/full.

4. David Brown, "Acetylcholine and Cholinergic Receptors," *Brain and Neuroscience Advances* 3 (December 2019), https://www.ncbi.nlm.nih.gov/pmc/articles/PMC7058246/.

5. Sourya Acharya and Samarth Shukla, "Mirror Neurons: Enigma of the Metaphysical Modular Brain," *Journal of Natural Science, Biology, and Medicine* 3, no. 2 (July 2012): 118–24, https://www.ncbi.nlm.nih.gov/pmc/articles/PMC3510904/.

6. Blaise Pascal, *Pensées* (Penguin Classics, 1995).

7. Nadia Whitehead, "People Would Rather Be Electrically Shocked Than Left Alone with Their Thoughts," *Science*, July 3, 2014, https://www.science.org/content/article/people-would-rather-be-electrically-shocked-left-alone-their-thoughts.

8. Carl Gustav Jung, *The Archetypes and the Collective Unconscious* (Princeton University Press, 1981), 23.

Chapter 4

1. Viren Swami, Samantha Hochstöger, Erik Kargl, and Stefan Stieger, "Hangry in the Field: An Experience Sampling Study on the Impact of Hunger on Anger, Irritability, and Affect," *PLoS One* 17, no. 7 (July 2022), https://doi.org/10.1371/journal.pone.0269629. See also, Alli Spotts-De Lazzer, "Scientific Proof That Being Hangry Is Real," *Psychology Today*, July 22, 2022, https://www.psychologytoday.com/us/blog/meaningfull/202207/scientific-proof-being-hangry-is-real.

2. Candice Myers, "Food Insecurity and Psychological Distress: A Review of the Recent Literature," *Current Nutritional Reports* 9,

no. 2 (June 2020): 107–18, https://www.ncbi.nlm.nih.gov/pmc/
articles/PMC7282962/.

3. Judith Glaser, "Your Brain is Hooked on Being Right," *Harvard
   Business Review*, February 28, 2013, https://hbr.org/2013/02/
   break-your-addiction-to-being#:~:text=In%20terms%20of%20
   its%20neurochemistry,building%2C%20and%20compassion%20
   shut%20down.

4. Daniel Kahneman with Olivier Sibony and Cass Sunstein, *Noise:
   A Flaw in Human Judgment* (Little, Brown Spark, 2021).

Chapter 5

1. Celeste Kidd and Benjamin Hayden, "The Psychology and
   Neuroscience of Curiosity," *Neuron* 88, no. 3 (Nov 2015): 440–60,
   https://www.ncbi.nlm.nih.gov/pmc/articles/PMC4635443/.

2. William James, *Talks to Teachers on Psychology: And to Students on
   Some of Life's Ideals* (Henry Holt, 1899), 45. 1899 was the original
   publication year and it has since been reprinted.

3. Douglas Ready, "In Praise of the Incurably Curious Leader," *MIT
   Sloan Management Review*, July 18, 2019, https://sloanreview.mit.
   edu/article/in-praise-of-the-incurably-curious-leader/.

4. Matt Pressman, "Elon Musk Cites 'Obsessive Curiosity' as Most
   Important Daily Habit," CleanTechnica, November 22, 2022,
   https://cleantechnica.com/2022/11/22/elon-musk-cites-obsessive-
   curiosity-as-most-important-daily-habit/.

5. Joyce Shaffer, "Neuroplasticity and Clinical Practice: Building
   Brain Power for Health," *Frontiers in Psychology* 7 (July 2016),
   https://www.ncbi.nlm.nih.gov/pmc/articles/PMC4960264/.

6. Harvard University Press, "Lincoln's Reading Habits."

7. Shaffer, "Neuroplasticity and Clinical Practice."

8. Katsuhiko Miyazaki, Kayoko W. Miyazaki, Akihiro Yamanaka,
   Tomoki Tokuda, Kenji F. Tanaka, and Kenji Doya, "Reward

Probability and Timing Uncertainty Alter the Effect of Dorsal Raphe Serotonin Neurons on Patience," *Nature Communications* 9 (2018), https://www.nature.com/articles/s41467-018-04496-y.

Chapter 6

1. Mohandas Gandhi, *Gandhi: An Autobiography: The Story of My Experiments with Truth*, with Mahadev H. Desai (translator) and Sissela Bok (foreword) (Beacon Press, 1993). This the "authorized American edition." See also, Martin Luther King, Jr., *Autobiography of Martin Luther King, Jr.*, ed. Clayborne Carson (Warner Books, 1998). First trade printing 2001 by the estate of his heirs.

2. Tony Bacon, "Interview: Paul McCartney on His Life as a Bassist," Reverb, January 11, 2018, https://reverb.com/news/interview-paul-mccartney-on-his-life-as-a-bassist.

3. Arun Starkey, "The Two Bassists That Influenced Paul McCartney" *Far Out Magazine*, February 14, 2022, https://faroutmagazine.co.uk/two-bassists-influenced-paul-mccartney/.

4. Brené Brown, *Daring Greatly: How the Courage to Be Vulnerable Transforms the Way We Live, Love, Parent, and Lead* (Avery, 2012), 45.

5. Jim Collins, *Good to Great: Why Some Companies Make the Leap . . . And Others Don't* (HarperBusiness, 2001), 20.

6. *Gandhi*, directed by Richard Attenborough, written by John Briley (1982; Goldcrest Films).

7. Mark 10:22 (ESV).

8. Matthew 11:11 (ESV).

9. John 3:30 (ESV).

INDEX

INDEX

INDEX

ABOUT THE AUTHOR

Bob Galindo Jr. is a third- and sometimes fourth-degree follower (always in progress) who has spent his life striving to learn how to follow with reason—falling and getting up again and again, striving for that elusive fifth degree of vulnerability. With more than thirty years of experience in the investment advisory industry, he has been fortunate to achieve professional success in leadership positions, retiring in 2018 as the principal financial officer and treasurer of a prominent $80 billion mutual fund company. A United States Navy veteran, Bob earned his bachelor's and master's degrees at the University of Texas at San Antonio (Go Runners!). In addition to writing countless business, regulatory, and financial reports, Bob has authored op-eds and even recorded some music. He is a talented public speaker and has also appeared on stage as a professional musician, vocalist, and musical theater performer.

www.ingramcontent.com/pod-product-compliance
Lightning Source LLC
Chambersburg PA
CBHW031854200326
41597CB00012B/413